Wo..d
from
Word

Saturation in the Word of God
from 1 John 1:1-9

Stephen Manley

Cross Style Press™

Word From Word: 1 John 1:1-9
Copyright © Stephen Manley, 2013

Edited by Delphine Manley

ISBN: 978-0615811796

Word From Word (1 John 1:1-9) was originally published as seven separate volumes.

Additional copies may be ordered from:
    Cross Style Global Ministries
    PO Box 2089
    Lebanon, TN 37088

    www.CrossStyle.org

Introduction

Please read this introduction several times. Please continue to read it to begin your saturation for each day. It is imperative these concepts rest in your mind.

1. This is not an academic pursuit! We are not attempting to gain knowledge or accumulate facts. How much or how long is not the issue. We are not on a schedule (except His). SO RELAX!

2. Why are we doing this? What do we want to accomplish? We are seeking Jesus! Not Jesus the idea, concept, or doctrine. We are pursuing the person of Christ. We are coming to the Scriptures for the revelation of His person. This is an attempt to embrace Him tighter.

3. The superior, supreme method of seeking Him is to listen to Him talk. The Scripture is not an ancient document which must come under critical analysis. It is the parting of the lips of Christ who is speaking these words to you now. It is fresh and new as this very day. Be careful for the ink on the page of your Bible may smear. It has not had time to dry.

4. I am not a student; therefore how can I study the Scriptures? This is not on an intellectual level. The Author Himself indwells you. He alone can explain what He is saying. Will you listen to Him?

5. There is no special study technique or method. We are going to give the Author time to speak to us. This will not be done by setting aside several hours a day to do research in the Scriptures. We are going to saturate. We are going to spend all day investigating the Word of God. We will begin our day

with a focus for our saturation. We will investigate words and phrases as we have time. But above this we will ponder the passage of our focus all day. We will seek His face in the passage. This will happen while at our job, eating our dinner, or walking down the street. What He has to say to us will be the focus for our day.

6. If your saturation for one day on a passage does not seem adequate, do not hurry and move on to another verse. Stay in the passage on which you are saturating until you sense the material has compelled you. Remember we are discovering Him!

Let's begin!!!!!!!!!!!!

Word

from

Word

Part One
1 John 1:1-2

Day 1

Our first task will be to look at the first section John gives us in his first chapter. It includes the first four verses. We are going to construct an outline of the entire book so we can easily see the sections of the book and how they fit together. Our outline begins like this:

    I. Introduction (1:1-4)
      A. The Person (1:1, 2)
      B. The Purpose (1:3, 4)

Read the section focused on the Person. Spend time writing these two verses on a card you can carry in your pocket. Every time you have opportunity through the day read these verses. You are reading these verses to discover the Person. On the back of the card record beginning notes on who He is!

Day 2

Now that you have spent a day with the first two verses, we need to recognize the first three verses make up one long sentence. It is a very difficult sentence to diagram. Add the third verse to your written card containing the first two verses. Your single task today in saturation will be to discover the subject of this long sentence. About what does everything in this sentence point to and speak?

Day 3

From your saturation yesterday you should have discovered the subject of the entire sentence of verses one, two, and three is *That which*.   It is a translation from a Greek relative pronoun. In your saturation you should have discovered the antecedent or content of this pronoun is *the Word of life*. From the very beginning phrase *That which was from the beginning,* we realize John is relating back to the beginning of his Gospel account.   You should become familiar with John 1:1-5. Nouns have gender. *Word* is in the masculine gender. One can easily understand this because it is a reference to Christ.   However the unique thing is that the Greek word translated *That which* is in the neuter gender. This suggests that the content and quality of the Word can not clearly be described in human language.   The author is attempting to take us beyond the comprehension of our languages. He is indicating we will not be able to adequately describe the Person we are discussing. This gives us reason for the length and details of this sentence in which we are saturating.   In your saturation today, allow the Lord to reveal John 1:1-5 and 1 John 1:1 to you.   Allow Him to impress upon you the largeness of what is happening in Christ for your sake!

Day 4

We want to saturate today in the phrase *concerning the Word of Life*. Everything in this large sentence is an expression of this phrase. This phrase does not appear anywhere else in the New Testament which gives it a high standing in this passage. Let's saturate in the words as they appear in the phrase:

Concerning – The Greek word often expresses the central point from which an action proceeds or from which it is exerted. In this sense John is saying everything I am describing in the rest of the sentence comes from *the Word of life*.

the Word – This is the major word in this phrase. As noted before it has definite reference back to John 1:1-5. Before anything has ever been there was the "idea." Someone in their mind has an idea and from the idea an item is formed. This is the concept of *the Word*. God had an idea of all He wanted for mankind. How man was to live, the form of his character, the depth of his mind and understanding, and the expression of all of the above were all an idea in the mind of God. Jesus is that idea brought to reality. All God wants for you is contained in *the Word*.

of life – This noun gives content to the main noun, *Word*. Thus it is the Word which gives life or is life, or causes people to live. There are several different Greek words which can be translated life. The Greek word here does not refer to the soul of man or to the biological life of man. Rather it refers to vitality, the (not essentially personal) principle and force of life, animating man's motion and action, his intellect and emotions. Thus the *Word* is the generating sourcing of our total life expression.

Saturate on these things today!

Day 5

To adequately understand the elements of these verses, we must saturate on the aspect of the time element. Think carefully about what time period is covered in this one great sentence. There are actually three distinct time periods. What are these tree time periods?

1 John 1:1-2
Day 6

From yesterday's saturation you should have discovered the following time periods:

1. The Distant Past – John is definitely taking us back to the very beginning of things. He states *That which was from the beginning*. We will want to do a thorough study of this concept. Also notice in verse two he states, *that eternal life which was with the Father and was manifested to us*.

2. The Disciples' Past – This refers to the period of time the disciples were with Christ. John states it clearly in verse one, *which we have heard, which we have seen with our eyes, which we have looked upon, and our hands have handled*. He continues with statements such as *we have seen* (1:2), *we have seen and heard* (1:3).

3. The Derived Present – This includes all of the rest of the verses not in the above. These words are being declared to us at this moment in this day.

Our saturation today will be in taking these three time periods and applying them to our lives. What does the Distant Past have to do with you? Place yourself in the shoes of the Disciples' Past. What has God allowed you to see, handle, and now declare? The Derived Present brings us into this moment. What is He saying to you now?

Day 7

Remember the subject of this long sentence was the pronoun translated *That which*. It referred to *the Word of life*. Refresh this idea in your mind. Now let's move to the verb *was*. I want to present to you two Greek words to think about today in your saturation. One of them is the word "ginomai." This is used in the prologue of John's Gospel. It can be translated "become." It is the equivalent of the middle passive of the Greek word "poieo." This word is translated "do" but is the kind of doing a tree is involved in when it bears fruit. It has to do with a creative flow from the inside. Always when Jesus is seen "doing," it is "poieo." There was the creative source of the Father through the Holy Spirit producing Him. It has the idea of coming into existence through the creative source.

Along with this is the Greek word "een" which is a part of our saturation today. It is the imperfect form of "to be" or "am." The imperfect means there was something in the past which has continuous effect into the present. The Greek word translated *was* is "een." In this passage it leaves us with the emphasis of eternal. Also this verb is in the active voice which means the subject is responsible for its action.

Saturate in the first two verses in light of this concept. Contrast this concept with the idea of "ginomai." See each phrase in light of "een."

Day 8

Continue the saturation emphasis you started yesterday. Only today relate the prologue (John 1:1-18) of the Gospel of John with it. It reads like this:

In the beginning was (een) *the Word, and the Word was* (een) *with God, and the Word was* (een) *God. He was* (een) *in the beginning with God. All things were made* (ginomai) *through Him, and without Him nothing was made* (ginomai) *that was made* (ginomai). *In Him was* (een) *life, and the life was* (een) *the light of men. And the light shines in the darkness, and the darkness did not comprehend it. There was* (ginomai) *a man sent from God whose name was John. This man came for a witness, to bear witness of the Light, that all through him might believe. He was* (een) *not that Light, but was sent to bear witness of that Light. That was* (een) *the true Light which gives light to every man coming into the world. He was* (een) *in the world, and the world was made* (ginomai) *through Him, and the world did not know Him. He came to His own, and His own did not receive Him. But as many as received Him, to them He gave the right to become* (ginomai) *children of God to those who believe in His name: who were born, not of blood, nor of the will of the flesh, nor of the will of man, but of God. And the Word became* (ginomai) *flesh and dwelt among us, and we beheld His glory, the glory as of the only begotten of the Father, full of grace and truth. John bore witness of Him and cried out saying, "This was* (een) *He of whom I said, 'He who comes after me is preferred before me and He was* (een) *before me.'" And of His fullness we have all received and grace for grace. For the law was given through Moses, but grace and truth came* (ginomai) *through Jesus Christ. No one has seen God at any time. The only begotten Son, who is* (een) *in the bosom of the Father, He has declared Him.*

1 John 1:1-2

The subject of this three verse sentence is *That which*. This is a direct reference to *the Word of life*. Everything in these verses gives content to the Word of life. In your saturation today begin to make a list of this content.

We will want to form this into our outline when we finish with this section.

1 John 1:1-2

Day 10

No doubt the first thing on your list from yesterday's saturation is *from the beginning*. *The Word of life* is described as *from the beginning*. This phrase is used twice in the Gospel of John (John 8:44; 15:27). It is used nine times in this First Epistle of John (1 John 1:1; 2:7, 7, 13, 14, 24, 24; 3:8, 11). It is used two times in the Second Epistle of John (2 John 5, 6). Saturate in these various usages in order to glean how this phrase is used. Notice some times it is used absolutely (as in 1 John 2:13, 14; 3:8) and sometimes it is used relatively (as in John 15:27; 1John 2:24).

Day 11

There is a contrast established by John between the phrase *in the beginning* (John 1:1) and *from the beginning*. The phrase *in the beginning* is used by Moses to begin the Book of Genesis (1:1). Saturate today on the difference between these two phrases. Perhaps you will want to take a card and draw a line down the middle. On one side at the top write "in" and on the other side write "from." Throughout the day make a list of the difference.

1 John 1:1-2

Day 12

From your saturation yesterday you should have gleaned the following concept. The phrase *in the beginning* focuses on the initial point of creation. It looks back into eternity and describes that which was already in existence when creation began. John is telling us that the Word already present at the point of creation *in the beginning*. However the phrase *from the beginning* suggests what has been in existence from that moment of creation until now. In other words *in the beginning* characterizes the absolute Divine Word as He was before the foundation of the world and at the foundation of the world. *From the beginning* characterizes the development the revelation of His person in time.

It is also interesting to note that the article is not present in both phrases in original Greek writing. We have inserted it in our English translation. This presents *the beginning* not as a definite, concrete fact, but *the beginning* as seen through the eyes of man. It has to do with that to which we look as *beginning*.

Saturate today in the application of this to your life. You are embracing the One who is both *in the beginning* and *from the beginning*.

1 John 1:1-2

Remember your list of items which give content to *the Word of life*? No doubt the first on the list was *from the beginning*. Now let's go to the second one in verse one. It is *we have heard*. There is a stronger emphasis in the New Testament on hearing than on seeing. Notice hearing is listed first in this verse.

What Jesus looked like is of little significance. What He said is of great importance. He is *the Word of life*. The Greek word translated *we have heard* is in the perfect tense. This refers to an event which happened in the past but has continuing results in the present. Saturate today on the content of what they had heard.

1 John 1:1-2

Day 14

The next phrase for our consideration is *we have seen with our eyes*. However, this must be compared with the following phrase, *we have looked upon*. These are translations of two different Greek words. These same two words are used in the opening chapter of John's Gospel account. Look at John 1:14 and John 1:18. The Greek word translated *we have seen* (1 John 1:1) is used in verse eighteen (John 1:18). The Greek word translated *we have looked upon* (1 John 1:1) is used in verse fourteen (John 1:14). Saturate in the comparisons to discover the significance of the usage.

Day 15

The difference between the Greek Word translated *we have seen* and the Greek Word translated *we have looked upon* is remarkable. *We have seen* emphasizes the fact of "face to face." *We have looked upon* carries with it the idea of "to wonder." One scholar translates it "a spectacle which broke on our astonished vision." John is relating back to the days when he was with Christ. Can you relate this kind of experience to your relationship with Christ? Let this dominate your thoughts today!

1 John 1:1-2

Day 16

In your saturation you may have noticed the number of times the word *which* has appeared. The subject of the sentence is *that which*. It is a translation of one Greek word. This is the same Greek word which is translated *which* three other times in verse one. In the original Greek language it is included one more time before the phrase *our hands have handled* although it is not seen in our translation. Note the rhythm of the verse.

This pronoun is in the neuter gender and its antecedent, *the Word of life*, is in the masculine gender. This is the author's way of suggesting the idea is bigger than can be expressed in our language. When this Greek word is used the first time in the sentence as the subject it is in the nominative case. The other three times it is used it is in the accusative case. It is what is called an adverbial accusative. It is used to indicate various types of directions or limitations on the verb's actions with respect to time, place, things, and manner of behavior. You will remember the verb is *was*. It is a translation of "een." It has to do with pre-existence or eternal. Think of what John is saying. He has had the opportunity of hearing, seeing, looking upon that which is pre-existent and eternal. Saturate in this today.

1 John 1:1-2

Day 17

There is one more phrase in verse one of chapter one on which we need to saturate. It is *and our hands have handled*. See this phrase as a climax to all that has gone before. The term *hands* is often used to refer to, or to emphasize, agency. In other words *hands* are an agent of the entire person of the disciple. John is emphasizing the senses of the disciples. They heard, saw, and touched. The Greek word translated *have handled* is also used in the resurrection appearance of Christ in the upper room (Luke 24:39). No doubt John was thinking of those kind of experiences. Saturate in verse one as a whole. See it from the climax of the most personal involvement of touching. Let it increase your desire to have this kind of relationship with Him.

1 John 1:1-2

Day 18

Today in our saturation, let's go back to the development of our outline for the book.   You will remember the outline for these first four verses is

> I. Introduction (1:1-4)
>   A. The Person (1:1, 2)
>   B. The Purpose (1:3, 4)

Let's add some detail under the section "A.   The Person (1:1, 2)." Organize the material as point "1." and "2." under section "A."   Notice there is no right and wrong to this. Saturate on this today.

Day 19

Let me suggest to you the following outline for our passage:

   I. Introduction (1:1-4)
      A. The Person (1:1, 2)
         1. Past to the Present (1:1a)
         2. Physical Testimony (1:1b)
      B. The Purpose (1:3, 4)

Let's begin our saturation focused on verse two. You will notice in our translation there is a dash at the end of verse one and one at the end of verse two. Other translations give this same effect by putting parenthesis around the verse. This means it is an insert verse given to us for further explanation.

John ended verse one with the phrase *the Word of life*. Now he is going to give additional content to this phrase. He is saying, "Let me give you more information on the life I just mentioned." In your saturation notice he modifies this subject by adding the word *eternal*.

The Greek word translated *was manifested* means to make apparent, manifest, known, show openly. Notice the correspondence between the phrase *the life was manifested* and *the Word became flesh* (John 1:14). *The Word became flesh* focuses simply on the great historical fact of the incarnation. *The life was manifested* presents the revelation of that truth in the daily operations of life. The one proclaims the objective process of the incarnation as such, the other points to the results of that process as related to human capacity of receiving and understanding it. It has been said, "The reality of the incarnation would be undeclared if it were said, 'The Word was manifested;' the manifoldness of the operations of life would be circumscribed if it were said, 'The Life became flesh.' The manifestation of the Life was a consequence of the incarnation of the Word, but it is not coextensive with it" (Westcott).

Do you see the completeness of what we have in Christ? He is not a moment, an experience. He is a lifestyle. He is not a vision to be remembered, but an embracing of our lives for every day. Let these things grip you today!

1 John 1:1-2

Our saturation today focuses on the verb tenses of verse two. Remember this is an insert verse giving content and explanation of what has been said in verse one. He has told us about *the Word of life*. He will now continue with the explanation of this *life*.

The first verb is *was manifested*. It is in the aorist tense. We usually translated this tense in the past tense. Here is something which happened in a period of time in the past. The focus is on the happening. The second verb is *have seen*. This is in the perfect tense. It tells of an event in the past which has continuous effect in the present. The third verb is *bear witness*. It is in the present tense. The fourth verb is *declare* which is in the present tense. Does this not give us a flow of what ought to be happening in our lives? Revelation has come to us! We have embraced it and are being affected even this moment by it! Do we not need to bear witness and declare it?

1 John 1:1-2

Day 21

It is very significant in this insert, explanation verse (verse 2) the last three verbs (*have seen, bear witness, declare*) focused on *that eternal life*. It is the goal of all three of these verbs. It is as if since He has been manifested, there is nothing else beyond Him. *We have seen.* Remember this verb is in the perfect tense. It refers to an event in the past which has continuous results into this present moment. The revelation was so huge; it has dominated us to this moment. He has so captivated us there is nothing but the reality of His person within us. Saturate on this concept!

Bear witness and *declare* are the present tense manifestation of what *we have seen.* What else would you expect? If something in the past is so big it has dominated us into the present, would it not be the constant revelation of our entire lives?

1 John 1:1-2

Day 22

Let's saturate on the ideas of *bear witness* and *declare*. *Bear witness* is a legal term for telling in the courts what a person has seen or heard. It is the same basic root Greek word used by Jesus when He said, *"But you shall receive power when the Holy Spirit has come upon you; and you shall be witnesses to me in Jerusalem, and in all Judea and Samaria, and to the end of the earth,"* (Acts 1:8). It is interesting to note this word began to shift in meaning as the early church began to suffer persecution. It is the Greek word from which we get our English word "martyr." There was nothing light or superficial about this "bearing witness." This was the sole function of the apostles in the early church (Acts 1:22).

The meaning of *declare* is directly tied to the above, but is slightly different. In the Greek language it basically means "to report." Its primary definition is "to bring a message from any person or place." This is not the talent of exhortation. It is certainly not about expanding or making up ideas. It is the display of the exactness of the *eternal life*. Saturate on this concept!

1 John 1:1-2

Day 23

Let's saturate today on the phrase *which was with the Father and was manifested to us* (1 John 1:2).

The word *was* is again the Greek word "een." It has the idea of pre-existence or eternal. Again John is giving us the emphasis that the eternal life with which we have interacted had prior existence to our time.

As John describes Jesus to us, we discover He was with the Father. Who is the Father? All day long make notes on your card of what you know about the Father. Fill your mind and heart with the awareness of His being.

Day 24

Today we will continue our saturation on the phrase *which was with the Father and was manifested to us* (1 John 1:2). From your saturation yesterday your mind and heart should be overwhelmed with the essence of the Father.

Today we want to saturate in the concept of *with*. John is expressing the fact that the eternal life which he saw, understood, and declared was in linkage with the Father. The Greek word translated *with* has heavy meaning for us. The actual Greek word translated *with* implies motion or direction from a place. This indicates the idea of source, agent, or cause from which something comes or proceeds. It not only has the idea of motion or direction from but also towards. Thus it expresses dependence or relationship which has to do with belonging or pertaining to a person or thing. One scholar says that this word gives us "the preposition of motion with the verb of repose involving an eternity of relation with activity and life."

What is so important to understand is this Life eternally flowed to the Father, just as it emanated from Him. It came forth from Him and was manifested to the disciples (our world), but for the purpose that it might take us into itself and unite us with the Father. So the manifested Life (Christ) came from the Father in order to embrace us and carry us back to the Father.

Spend time on these thoughts! Thoroughly comprehend what John is saying in regard to *with*.

1 John 1:1-2

Day 25

We are continuing to saturate on the phrase *which was with the Father and was manifested to us* (1 John 1:2). Remember verse two is an insert section to give explanation. Focus today on the words *was manifested to us*. This is a repeat of the beginning of the verse (verse 2).

Compare the use of this word with other Scriptures. The same Greek Word translated *was manifested* is used also translated *He appears* (1 John 2:28). It is translated the same in Paul's writing to the Colossians (3:4). The Book of Hebrews also tells of this same appearing (9:26). Spend some time getting the impact of these verses. The word is used each time in the absolute sense. There is finality, completeness, accomplishment about the statement. See this as true in John's statement (1:2).

1 John 1:1-2

Day 26

We have worked out way through the first two verses of the first chapter of John's first epistle. In our saturation we need to review and make adequate application of the truth discovered. Remember the first three verses make up one sentence; therefore we have not completed the entire sentence. But the first two verses form the first section of our outline. Let's go back and review our outline of the epistle.

> I. Introduction (1:1-4)
>   A. The Person (1:1, 2)
>   B. The Purpose (1:3, 4)

Obvious everything we have done in our saturation has been focused on Jesus. In these first two verses John is highlighting the only thing he has to present. As an old man talking with his children (2:1), he is calling them back to the person of Christ. He is not correcting them about doctrine or church activities, but calling them to Christ. Let's saturate in the person of Christ today. Go over these two verses again and embrace Christ.

Day 27

Let's go back to our beginning outline for the book.

    I. Introduction (1:1-4)
        A. The Person (1:1, 2)
        B. The Purpose (1:3, 4)

You will remember when we finished saturating in the first verse, we added to our outline.

    I. Introduction (1:1-4)
        A. The Person (1:1, 2)
            1. Past to the Present (1:1a)
            2. Physical Testimony (1:1b)
        B. The Purpose (1:3, 4)

Now we want to add verse two to our outline.

    I. Introduction (1:1-4)
        A. The Person (1:1, 2)
            1. Past to the Present (1:1a)
            2. Physical Testimony (1:1b)
            3. ? ? ? ? ? ? ? ? ? ? (1:2)
        B. The Purpose (1:3, 4)

Saturate today in the overall view of verse two. What is the main thrust of his statement? Can you reduce it down to one word?

Day 28

One answer to yesterday's saturation might be "Proclamation."

I. Introduction (1:1-4)
    A. The Person (1:1, 2)
        1. Past to the Present (1:1a)
        2. Physical Testimony (1:1b)
        3. Proclamation (1:2)
    B. The Purpose (1:3, 4)

Saturate today on this question! How could there have been such a revelation as John has experienced without the result of **bear witness and declare to you** (1:2)? Does this kind of revelation not demand the witness? Apply this to your own personal life. Look at the large scope of the witness. It is the eternal Life of God which has captivated us. The focus is on the person of Christ. Is He properly represented in all phases of our life?

1 John 1:1-2

Day 29

Let's return to verse one today for our saturation and application. Obviously what we *bear witness* to and what we *declare* (1:2) is a direct result of what *we have heard*, what *we have seen with our eyes*, what *we have looked upon*, and what *our hands have handled*.

Perhaps the place to start is not witnessing techniques or presentations. Maybe what we need is not the development of a testimony. Maybe we need to see what we are hearing, seeing, looking upon, and handling. Is it not inevitable we will talk about and declare that which is dominate in our lives? This is not to propose we need to change our schedule. It is to propose we need to check on our focus. See nothing but Him today!

1 John 1:1-2

Day 30

Let's do this final day of applying verses one and two to our lives. While today is really important, note the emphasis of these two verses has an eternal ring to it. The phrase *from the beginning* is really important as an opening statement. Rediscover what this means. *The Word of life* is definitely linked with *that eternal life* which places the revelation to our lives in another bracket. Also the idea that this life *was with the Father and was manifested to us* brings us to awareness beyond our culture, traditions, and generation.

Today place your entire schedule within the realm of this kind of revelation. See how huge what God is doing really is! What is your response?

Word *from* Word

Part Two
1 John 1:3-4

1 John 1:3-4

Day 1

We have finished the first two verses of the first chapter which comprise the first section of our outline. Let's review the outline and see where the Word is taking us.

I. Introduction (1:1-4)
- A. The Person (1:1, 2)
    1. Past to the Present (1:1a)
    2. Physical Testimony (1:1b)
    3. Proclamation (1:2)
- B. The Purpose (1:3, 4)

Remember the first three verses make up one sentence. He has given a beautiful description of the person of Christ (1:1, 2). In verse one he made a bold statement. In verse two he gave an insert section. It gives explanation of the statement just made. Now he will finish out the sentence (1:3). Today you need to become familiar with the material. Take a card and write down verse three and four. Read them consistently throughout the day. Pray over them. Saturate!

1 John 1:3-4

Day 2

Remember the subject of this three verse sentence is *That which*. The antecedent to this pronoun is *Word of life*. In these first two verses John has been giving the detailed involvement he has had in that One he is declaring to us. Notice the phrase *we have seen* is being used for the third time. Notice the phrase *we have heard* is being used for the second time and will be used the third time in 1 John 1:5.

Now in verse three as he finishes this long sentence and on into verse four, John is going to give us the purpose for the declaration. Saturate to discover the purpose. Be sure and see the purpose in its details.

1 John 1:3-4

Day 3

Let's begin an investigation of the purpose on which you saturated yesterday. No doubt you discovered the focus of the purpose is *to you*. John writes *that which we have seen and heard we declare to you* (1 John 1:3). He is going to emphasize this again by making you the subject of the purpose clause which begins with *that*. The first time John uses it this pronoun is in the dative case. This serves as a direct object. In other words, the one who is going to receive the action of the revelation is *you*. Notice he has shifted from the use of *we* to *you*. Now the revelation has come to us. Saturate on this powerful truth today. All of the revelation of Jesus which came to John as an eyewitness is now coming to you. Would you allow Jesus to reveal Himself to you today?

1 John 1:3-4

Day 4

We want to focus on the purpose clauses today. There is one purpose clause given in verse three and another purpose clause given in verse four. A purpose clause can be easily discovered because it begins with the word "that," "because," or "so." In verse three he writes *that you also may have fellowship with us; and truly our fellowship is with the Father and with His Son Jesus Christ.* In verse four he states *that your joy may be full.* Compare these two phrases. How do they relate to each other? How are they in contrast? Saturate!

1 John 1:3-4

Day 5

You will want to keep your notes from yesterday's saturation at hand for the next few days. You may want to make some adjustments or additions as you saturate on these two purpose clauses. The first purpose clause is *that you may have fellowship with us.* The verb of the clause is *may have.* It is one word in the Greek language. It is in the subjunctive mood. The idea of this mood is "if," "conditional," or "when." John is saying, "I really want this to happen for you, but I can not guarantee it. There are conditions involved!" Saturate on the conditional aspect of the verse. What are the conditions according to the passage?

1 John 1:3-4

Day 6

Perhaps the answer to the question on which you saturated yesterday is found in the main idea of the purpose clause. The purpose clause is *that you may have fellowship with us*. Is not the main idea *fellowship*? Spend your time today saturating on this main idea. This is one of the main thoughts of the entire epistle. It comes from the Greek word "koinonia." It is a word used strongly by the Apostle Paul for the body of Christ, the church. It has the idea of partners, partakers, or associates. It is much more than just being at a party for an evening and having good fellowship. One in fellowship is engaged in an enterprise with another. It is definitely a relational term. In light of this scan the entire first chapter of this epistle and notice the times the word *fellowship* is used. Include these in your saturation.

Let's continue in our saturation of the main idea of this first purpose clause, *fellowship*. Since this is one of the main themes of this epistle it is critical that we have a good grasp on this concept. We want to see this concept in light of the rest of the Scriptures, but we must continually come back to our basic Scripture in this epistle or we will lose sight of our overall saturation.

This word, *fellowship* (koinonia), is used in a business sense in Luke 5:10. It has to do with the enterprise of fishing. In 2 Corinthians 8:23, it is used to describe a partnership within the enterprise of ministry. Write both of these verses on a card and saturate on them today. Bring this into the context of our passage in 1 John 1:3!

1 John 1:3-4

Day 8

Let's continue in our saturation of this main idea of *fellowship*. Let the concept discovered yesterday continue to influence your thought. Fellowship is not just having a good time together, but partners in the sense of joining in a great enterprise.

Paul describes this same concept in relation to a critical issue in the early church at Corinth. He was dealing with the issue of buying the cheap meat which had been offered to idols. He makes it very plain that idols are nothing (1 Corinthians 10:19). There is no life in them and they have no effect at all. This is also true with the meat which has been offered to them. It is simply meat. The issue is far beyond the idol and the meat. He explains that the Gentiles are making *sacrifice to demons and not to God* (1 Corinthians 10:20). He then pronounces the crucial issue: *I do not want you to have fellowship* (partnership, koinonia) *with demons. You cannot drink the cup of the Lord and the cup of demons; you cannot partake* (synonym of koinonia) *of the Lord's table and the table of demons* (1 Corinthians 10:20, 21).

It is interesting when living in sin we thought we did what we chose to do. After all it was our life. We responded to our body drives and what pleased our spirits. All the time we had entered into "partnership" with demons! We were a part of the Satanic enterprise. We were aggressive business partners fulfilling the dreams and desires of the Devil. In our own self-centered will, we were drawn into intimate fellowship with the demonic person. It is horrifying to consider. Saturate on your personal involvement in koinonia. Be sure and relate this to our passage in 1 John 1:3.

1 John 1:3-4

Day 9

Yesterday we saturated on the negative aspect of *fellowship*. Today lets saturate on the very opposite, the positive. The Apostle Peter gives us the very opposite picture of "partnership." He begins his second epistle by speaking of the great Divine power of God. This power is the Author of all things that pertain to life and godliness (2 Peter 1:3). It is through this very power that *precious promises* have been put in place. Through these promises which are the expression of the very heart's desire of God *you may be partakers* (koinonia) *of the divine nature, having escaped the corruption that is in the world through lust* (2 Peter 1:4). We have entered into a partnership with the very heart of God. His burning heart's enterprise has become ours. We are in intimate fellowship with what makes Him who He is!

Write these verses from Peter's epistle down on a card and saturate on them today. Be sure and relate the concept back to our main passage in 1 John 1:3.

1 John 1:3-4

Day 10

Let's continue in our saturation on the concept of *fellowship*. We have looked at the negative aspect and yesterday on the positive aspect. Do you see the Bible only considers two kinds of partnerships? There seem to be only two possibilities for your life. You are either going to be a partner with Satan, fulfilling his dreams, engaged in his enterprise or you will be in partnership with Christ. You will be filled with His nature, involved in His plans, knowing His heart or you will be possessed with demonic nature, accomplishing his ends, and embracing his heart. There is no third category. The concept of neutrality does not exist. There is not even a half and half.

Relate this concept to our passage in 1 John 1:3. Notice how he expands this as he continues into verses 6 and 7.

1 John 1:3-4

Day 11

Are you becoming aware of the powerful factor that this *fellowship* is the heart of the Scriptures? The purpose of the writing of this First Epistle of John is to bring us into *fellowship* with God.

The writer of the Book of Hebrews tells us how this possibility has been presented to us. In so doing, he gives an illustration of the actual union with God which can be experienced. He tells us of Christ. *Inasmuch then as the children have partaken* (form of koinonia) *of flesh and blood, He Himself likewise shared in the same, that through death He might destroy him who had the power of death, that is, the devil* (Hebrews 2:14). A son has become a partner with the very nature of his father, so Jesus has become a partner with our humanity. The Greek word translated *shared* is a synonym of "koinonia." God has become flesh. Thus the incarnation is an illustration of the kind of partnership God is offering to us. In fact, the Hebrew author is telling us the reason why God has done this. He is destroying the devil who has the power of death. One partnership is being eliminated for the sake of another partnership. Is this happening in your life?

Saturate on this passage in the Book of Hebrews and it is related to 1 John 1:3.

1 John 1:3-4

Day 12

Let's continue in our saturation of the concept of fellowship. Paul expressed this through the concept of grafting. *And if some of the branches were broken off, and you, being a wild olive tree, were grafted in among them, and with them became a partaker* (form of koinonia) *of the root and fatness of the olive tree* (Romans 11:17). Paul is emphasizing the close participation of the engrafted branch in the total life of the cultivated olive. It is a partnership in a great enterprise. It is far beyond just being "a part" or receiving benefits. It is actually experiencing the life giving sap of the tree. It is being a vital part of the great business of the tree. With the branch the tree can not fulfill its natural desire. Oh, to be grafted into Christ in such a way. Is it possible to become such a partner to the Divine? We become the fulfillment of His very heart's desire!

Fill your life with these thoughts today. See this in light of our passage in 1 John 1:3.

1 John 1:3-4

Day 13

Let's spend one more day saturating on the concept of *fellowship*. Don't let any of these aspects of the partnership escape you. They give us content to our passage in 1 John 1:3.

Paul is so strong on this mystical union with Christ. He states, *God is faithful, by whom you were called into the fellowship* (form of koinonia) *of his Son, Jesus Christ our Lord* (1 Corinthians 1:9). Our life is identified with Christ. We become partners in His death and resurrection. *I have been crucified with Christ; it is no longer I who live, but Christ lives in me; and the life which I now live in the flesh I live by faith in the Son of God, who loved me and gave Himself for me* (Galatians 2:20). The danger of this partnership seems to be in misunderstanding the union. Paul consistently clarifies the issue. *And our hope for you is steadfast, because we know that as you are partakers* (koinonia) *of the sufferings, so also you will partake of the consolation* (2 Corinthians 1:7). He has clearly stated the content of the suffering to which he refers. *For as the sufferings of Christ abound in us, so our consolation also abounds through Christ* (2 Corinthians 1:5).

To become a partner with Christ is the join Him in His life style. It is the life style of the cross! It is His enterprise, His business. But how else could it be? If we are grafted into the root, if we are partakers of the Divine nature would not the fruit be His? If we are business partners in the enterprise of His heart, would we not be an extension of that redemption? To join Him in His resurrection is to join Him in the fellowship of His suffering. To join Him on the deep level of His heart's concern is to partner with Him in the accomplishment of that concern.

I want to share with Him on this level. My heart must be joined together with His. I am surrendering the right to live my own life. I want Him to live His life through me. Wherever this take me, it will be fine. I must know intimacy with Him!

Take these verses stated by Paul and saturate on them today in light of 1 John 1:3.

Day 14

The first purpose clause for the declaration of the eyewitness of Christ is *that you also may have fellowship with us.* Notice however it does not stop there but continues to *and truly our fellowship is with the Father and with His Son Jesus Christ.* Saturate on bringing these two statements together. Why does he start with having *fellowship with us* and them move to having *fellowship* with God? Could this be the core truth of evangelism?

1 John 1:3-4

Day 15

That you also may have fellowship with us is the beginning of the first purpose clause. *You also* give reference to two categories of individuals. As seen in the passage, first there are those who were the actual eyewitnesses of the physical life of Christ. Secondly, there are those who are called to believe with out physically seeing. Thomas was absent from the upper room when the resurrected Lord first appeared to the disciples. Jesus graciously appeared to them again when Thomas was present. Because he stated that he could not believe unless he actually touched His hands and side, Thomas was invited to do so. Thomas then cried out *"My Lord and my God!" Jesus said to him, "Thomas, because you have seen Me, you have believed. Blessed are those who have not seen and yet have believed,"* (John 20:29). Obviously you and I are in this last group.

We are being invited to become partners with those who have actually seen Him. This will enable us to become partners with Him. The message the first group has to tell will enable us to believe and experience Christ. It is the process of evangelism. But notice it is more than just having fellowship or partnership with them. John is referring to actually entering into their fellowship or partnership. We are to become a part of the partnership they actually have and it is with the Father and with His Son. Our partnership with Christ is so close; no one can actually become a partner with us with out joining Him.

To whom are you becoming the first group? Saturate on this truth.

1 John 1:3-4

The truth upon which we saturated yesterday is clearly highlighted in two words. John begins the last phrase of verse three with *and*. The second word is *truly*. The emphasis of *and* is on the linkage to elements. *Truly* is a translation of the Greek word "de." Its primary translation is "but," "on the contrary," or "on the other hand." John is establishing a contrast. He is saying, "We really want you to become partners with us, but you must understand our partnership is with Him." He is strongly stating that you can not be engaged in partnership with us without realizing that partnership is with Christ.

This is what happened in the Book of Acts. Every person who came in contact on any level with the New Testament Christian soon realized he was in contact with Christ. There was no way of touching or engaging the Christian without engaging Christ. There were no aspects of the Christian's life that were not filled with Christ.

Again today saturate in applying this truth to your life.

1 John 1:3-4

Day 17

John writes *and truly our fellowship is with the Father and with His Son Jesus Christ.* In the Greek language John is writing this is his characteristic manner. He places an article (the) before the word *our*. "The fellowship, that which is ours" is a literal translation. He defines and emphasizes a noun by an article and a possessive pronoun. Notice this is not a personal pronoun but a possessive pronoun. This indicates the partnership or fellowship he is experiencing is not his alone (belonging to him) but is really a distinguishing mark of Christians. Every Christian will have this fellowship or partnership.

Saturate on this great truth. There is no way to be Christian without having fellowship, partnership, engagement in the great enterprise of the heart of God. This brings us back to the importance of intimacy with Christ.

1 John 1:3-4

Day 18

What kind of fellowship is being discussed? What is the content of the relationship? If it was actually happening what would it look like? Saturate in verse three today for the answer!

Remember saturation is not just having devotions in the morning. It is the involvement of the Word in your life all day long. As you saturate in the written Word you will find fellowship with the Living Word. Saturate the process in prayer.

1 John 1:3-4

Day 19

From your saturation yesterday, you should have noticed the strong phrase *with the Father and with His Son Jesus Christ*. One thing very apparent in the English as well as in the Greek text is the use of the word *with* twice. The repeated preposition *with* distinguishes the two persons. It implies the sameness of essence between the two and the fellowship which exists between the Father and Son. Thus the example of the kind of fellowship (partnership) into which we are being called is displayed for us. Saturate today on the intimacy between the Father and Son.

Write down and carry Jesus statement in Luke 2:49. He is twelve years old and has been separated from His parents in Jerusalem for five days. They have been looking for Him in Jerusalem for three full days. They come to the temple, no doubt to pray. Jesus is standing before them. They sternly quiz Him as any parent would. Jesus answers them, *"Did you not know that I must be about My Father's business?"* In the Greek text the word *business* is absent. The Greek word for *Father* is in the genitive case. This case is used to describe "relationship" between nouns or pronouns. In other words, Jesus must be involved in whatever is going on in His Father.

In the Parable of the Talents, the nobleman gave monies to ten servants. His instructions were *"Do business until I come!"* (Luke 19:13). The Greek word translated *business* means simply "to do business." They were not just to be servants, but to enter into the enterprise of the nobleman. This is the fellowship (koinonia) to which the Trinity is calling us.

Investigate such verses as John 5:19, 30. Carefully read the High Priestly Prayer of Jesus in John 17. Is it possible we are being drawn into the very fellowship (partnership) of the Trinity? The Trinity has not offered to us what He has but what He is. God has opened His heart to us and asked us to become partners (fellowship) with His heart.

1 John 1:3-4

Day 20

We are going to saturate on verse four today. John has stated purpose in verse three with a purpose clause beginning with the word *that*. Now in verse four he is going to give another purpose clause beginning with the same word. We want to discover if there is a different purpose involved or if he is simply restating the same purpose.

In addition don't over look the factor that the purpose is coming from something John is doing. Is he doing something different in this verse than he is doing in verse three?

This saturation will give us an overall view of the verse which is where we need to start.

Day 21

In the Greek text the first four Greek words are in this order –
Kai (and), tauta (these things), grafomen (write), heemeis (we).
He begins with the word *And*. It is stronger than simply
linking two equal ideas. It is used in the sense of consequence
or result. It might better be translated "therefore" or "so."
Therefore what I am going to state now is based upon what I
have already stated.

He is not simply restating the purpose already given in verse
three. He is wanting us to know the purpose of verse three (be
sure you are clear on this purpose) will result in the purpose of
verse four. We have not really studied the purpose as
described in verse four, but just from reading the words *that
your joy may be full* gives us enough indication to saturate all
day. It is as if even the purpose (verse three) has a purpose
(verse four). Note it is definitely redemptive and the
fellowship (koinonia – being a part of His enterprise) is not to
prosper Him but to prosper us.

1 John 1:3-4

Day 22

The second word in verse four in the Greek text (you will remember from yesterday) is translated *these things*. The significance of this statement seems to rest in the reference to the whole. He is not describing one single statement of what he has written up to this point; rather he is highlighting the entire epistle.

This is a very important emphasis in the concept of saturating. One must not saturate only in one verse or one section without considering the whole. In coming to a book like The First Epistle of John we attempt to discover the purpose of the whole writing. Everything in the book must be interpreted in light of this single purpose. It establishes the boundaries of the truth to be displayed. We are discovering this is the very first verses of this epistle. Be sure you understand his purpose for the writing of this whole epistle. Saturate on it today until it is absolutely clear. Go back over your notes from the previous days.

1 John 1:3-4

The third word in verse four in the Greek text is translated *write*. Go back in your notes and notice the Greek word. Is this not where we get our English word "graphic?" The ancient Greeks equated two Greek words. They are "graphoe" and "xeoe" (meaning to carve). This came from the fact that they original would carve figures with meaning on wooden tablets. These were later replaced when letters were developed. One engraved tablet was covered with another. They would be tied together and sealed, thus representing the form of an ancient letter. We conclude that the first literal writing was of this kind. For instance, God on Mt. Sinai carved the Ten Commandments into tablets of stone with His finger (Exodus 31:18). Therefore originally the word meant to cut in, make an incision. Later when parchment and paper began to be used, the meaning shifted to include writing. One can easily see how the idea of "it is written" became authoritative or permanently carved. Thus it denotes a legislative act or enactment.

Now bring this concept into what John is saying. It is interesting to note that the English translation of this phrase is *And these things we write to you*. In the Greek text the words *to you* are not there. This means the factor of *we write* is emphasized by the absence of *to you*. Notice that the content of the writing is stated clearly in verses one through three. It is a declaration of the **Word of life** which is the subject of the sentence in those verses. Jesus is the focus of the writing.

Day 24

The fourth word in verse four in the Greek text is *we*. Compare this to the change which takes place as you move into chapter two verses one, seven, and twelve through fourteen. Saturate on the reason for this shift and what is emphasized by it.

John is using the plural personal pronoun throughout the first five verses. It is definitely not his personal declaration, but it the message of the combined eyewitnesses who are urgently wanting to make Christ known. The partnership (koinonia) to which we are being invited is with the many who saw with their own eyes. But as wonderful as this is, the declaration of this epistle is going to come from John.

There is significant application about which to think. We are a part of the body of Christ, the church, which is making a strong statement to our world. But one must not hide within the group. The deciding factor for our lives is the personal declaration coming from our personal life and mouth.

1 John 1:3-4

Day 25

We are now ready to look at the actual purpose clause which is the reason for the writing. John states *that your joy may be full*. In the best Greek manuscripts, the Greek word translated *your* is seen as "our." It is not a great issue but gives us a renewed sense of how strong an impact this declaration is.

Throughout these four verses John is linking the many eyewitnesses, of which he is one, and those of us who have not see with the physical eyes. We are being drawn into the same fellowship (partnership, koinonia) *with Father and with His Son Jesus Christ*. Therefore the purpose of the writing is not just that your personal joy may be complete (although this is desired), but there is a completion of the joy of the entire body of Christ and the Trinity.

Saturate on the concept that it is necessary to win my fellowman to complete my personal joy as well as the joy of the body of Christ as well as the joy of the Trinity. John's writing indicates that the joy the eyewitnesses have because of their fellowship with God through Christ can be complete only when other individuals share that fellowship.

1 John 1:3-4

Day 26

The focus of the purpose clause for John's writing is the completion of *joy*. We need to carefully saturate on the content of this word. Joy is a delight of the mind. It is a positive consideration and mental condition. When moderate it is called gladness. When it is raised to the highest degree it is exultation. When our desires are limited by our possessions and we surrender, it is contentment. When our highest desires are accomplished, it is satisfaction. When battle rages and we win the victory, it is triumph. When joy has possessed our mind for so long it has settled into a pattern of the inner heart, we call it cheerfulness.

It was striking to study this concept in the context of the New Testament. There is a remarkable absence of the idea of happiness. In the beatitudes of Jesus (Matthew 5) a state of blessedness is described. This state seems to be completely beyond the level of happiness. The idea of joy and rejoice don't compare with being happy. There does not seem to be a Greek word which has as its primary translation the idea of being happy. The thrust of being happy seems to be a self-centered focus which is self-destructive. In other words, the very focus of desiring to be happy immediately destroys any possibility of it being experienced. Happiness seems to be a temporary emotion of the moment. It wavers with the circumstances of life. It seems to be connected with chance or luck. In fact, we make statements like "happy-go-lucky." Happiness is equated with no responsibilities which actually breeds the opposite.

Saturate today on the concept of joy not happiness. This seems to be the full intent of the Gospel presentation.

1 John 1:3-4

Read yesterday's notes again. Joy is distinctly different than happiness. The use of the word "joy" or "rejoice" in the Old Testament is very revealing. The most frequently used Hebrew word is translated into the English words "joy," "gladness," or "mirth." It is used in the Book of Proverbs in a powerful statement. The author states, **The light of the righteous rejoices, But the lamp of the wicked will be put out,** (Proverbs 13:9).

Here it properly means "to be bright" or "to shine." Joy is connected with righteousness and the demonstration of the brilliant glory as it is lived out. There are other Hebrew nouns which are translated "exult," "rejoice," "joy," or "shouting." They actually come from the root word which is a verb meaning "to go in a circle," "to be excited," or "to dance around for joy." Note in the Hebrew language the idea of joy is expressed in a full body demonstration.

Saturate on the connection between *joy* and the *fellowship* (koinonia). The purpose clause for the declaration in the first three verses is focused on *fellowship*. The purpose clause for the writing in verse four is focused on the completion of *joy*.

1 John 1:3-4

Day 28

The concept of *joy* is dominant in the writings of John. Today copy the following verses on a card and saturate on them in connection with verse four.

Look at John 15:11. It is used in connection with the Parable of the Vine and Branches. See the concept of *fellowship* (koinonia) within that relationship. The vine and branches are linked in a great enterprise.

Look at John 16:20, 22, and 24. Notice these statements are the climax of a discourse which begins in chapter fourteen and continues through chapter sixteen. The single subject of this discourse is the ascension of Christ and the sending of the Promise of the Father. The disciples are going to be filled with the Holy Spirit. The Parable of the Vine and the Branch is a physical illustration of this filling. Again be very much aware of the issue of *fellowship* (koinonia) in this experience.

Look at John 17:13. This is the High Priestly Prayer of Jesus. Notice the reference of the coming to the Father and the declaration of truth in the world resulting in *joy*.

1 John 1:3-4

Day 29

In verse four, the Greek word for *joy* is "chara." It actually comes from the root word "chairo" which means "rejoice." Saturate today on the comparison between these two Greek words and the Greek word "charis" which is "grace."

Notice the procedure of the words is backwards. I thought the basic root word would be "charis" (grace). From this basic word would come "chara" (joy) and "chairo" (rejoice). The grace of God would produce great joy resulting in rejoicing. But the root word is "chairo" (rejoice). From this state of rejoicing comes the condition of "chara" (joy) and "charis" (grace).

We are being called upon to become partners (koinonia) with the very nature of God. Within the nature of God there is the great activity of rejoicing. This state enabled Him to flow forth with grace which is the basis of all redemption. If I am filled with rejoicing (the nature of God) I will live in a state of forgiveness to all and find joy.

1 John 1:3-4

Day 30

Add one more factor to *your joy*. It is *that your joy may be full*. The Greek word is "pepleeroomenee." It means "to make full." It expresses that the joy will lack nothing, that it will fill their hearts to the brim. The term refers to the highest degree: they will be as glad as they possibly can be. This is to be a state of living for us.

Let's go back and reconstruct the outline we have been following. Saturate on the outline and allow each section of truth to come back to your memory as you view these four introductory verses.

    I. Introduction (1:1-4)
        A. The Person (1:1, 2)
            1. Past to the Present (1:1a)
            2. Physical Testimony (1:1b)
            3. Proclamation (1:2)
        B. The Purpose (1:3, 4)
            1. (of the) Proclamation (1:3)
                a. Partnership with us (1:3)
                b. Partnership with Father (1:3)
                c. Partnership with His Son (1:3)
            2. (of the) Printing (1:4)
                a. Pepleerooménee (1:4)
                b. Pleasurable Contentment (1:4)

Word

from

Word

Part Three
1 John 1:5

1 John 1:5

Day 1

We have finished John's introduction and are ready to begin the first of five major sections to this great epistle. Let's prepare ourselves for the launch into this great material. I would insist on you reading the statement on page one. I realize you have already become familiar with the material, but it is essential to focus on these principles.

This first major section of study is chapter one beginning at verse five through the end of the chapter which is verse ten. Read these verses several times. Take the time to write down on a card verses five through seven. Fill your saturation today in dwelling on these verses again and again. Attempt to see the major theme of this section.

1 John 1:5

Day 2

No doubt from yesterday's saturation you arrived at the conclusion that the major theme of this section is *fellowship*. Everything John says in this entire section (1 John 1:5-10) is about *fellowship*. In fact, we are going to discover through saturation that the rest of the book is going to focus on this theme.

In your saturation today, go back and review verses three and four of this chapter. In this "Introduction" we titled this section "The Purpose (1:3, 4)." Tie this statement of the purpose of the entire book with the theme of our present study (1 John 1:5-7).

You may need to go back and review your saturation on the word *fellowship* from verse three. If this is the entire subject of the book of 1 John we will want to constantly refer to this word and its content. Everything John says from this point on must be interpreted in light of this concept.

In your saturation today focus on this meaning of fellowship. Allow your review of this concept to refresh this experience in your own life. Select some key phrases or words which will help in the future to remind you of the content of this word.

Consider the word "koinonia."
Consider the involvement of "partnership."
Consider the greatness of the "enterprise."
Consider the issue of "intimacy."

Day 4

In our saturation today we want to specifically note how *fellowship* is highlighted in these verses. How would you state it? First note the idea of *fellowship* as seen in the theme of the entire section (1 John 1:5-10). Is he not giving us the heart of that fellowship? Is he not presenting to us the very condition or qualification if one is going to enter into such an enterprise of intimacy with God? What word best states this idea?

Let's go back to our basic outline. Remember this is not a right or wrong but what helps you to comprehend and pinpoint the truth of the passage. So you may want to choose other words than I might use.

    I. Introduction (1:1-4)
        A. The Person (1:1, 2)
           1. Past to the Present (1:1a)
           2. Physical Testimony (1:1b)
           3. Proclamation (1:2)
        B. The Purpose (1:3, 4)
           1. (of the) Proclamation (1:3)
              a. Partnership with us (1:3)
              b. Partnership with Father (1:3)
              c. Partnership with His Son (1:3)
           2. (of the) Printing (1:4)
              a. Pepleerooménee (1:4)
              b. Pleasurable Contentment (1:4)

Let's add to our outline this next section:

    II. The Platform for Fellowship (1:5-10)

Day 5

In our saturation today we want to take the major section (The Platform for Fellowship) found in the rest of the chapter (1 John 1:5-10) and carefully divide it into two sections. The first section (1:5-7) has already been the focus of your saturation. The second section is obviously the rest of the chapter (1:8-10). How do these two sections compare? What is the progression he is revealing to us? How does the second section build on the first section? Can you think of key words to describe this which would fit into our outline? These must be words which embody the truth being presented.

1 John 1:5

Day 6

From our saturation yesterday we want to expand our outline. This will give us guidance in our interpretation of the passage as we get into the details. Again remember it is not right and wrong but comprehension.

The first section (1:5-7) is calling us into *fellowship* with the God who is *light*. The contrast is between *light* and *darkness*. But note he is not focusing on an experience of *light* such as Saul of Tarsus had (Acts 9:3). He uses words like *walk* and *practice*. We will saturate on these words at a later time, but obviously he is referring to our daily living. This *light* is to be the flow of our life day in and day out! What word would be appropriate to describe this for our outline?

The second section (1:8-10) is a discussion of what has been suggested from the end of verse seven. Notice he states a progression in the first section. He goes from the concept of *darkness* (1:5, 6) to the idea of *lie and do not practice the truth* (1:6). He then moves into the idea of *sin* (1:7). This is the content of *darkness* which is the opposite of *light*. This second section (1:8-10) is going to highlight this concept. He is going to give us specific instruction on exactly how to respond to *sin* and what is required to move us from this *darkness* into the *light*. What word would be appropriate to describe this for our outline?

Let's look at the conclusions from yesterday's saturation. The purpose of that saturation was to give us an over all view of the passage. This is significant before we investigate the details of exactly what he is saying. This is important in order to establish the boundary of what he is expressing which will guide us in our interpretation.

Again do not get "hung up" on terms or individual words. We are anxious to grasp the concept of his communication. The reason for individual words is to help us remember and know at a glance what he is saying. We have entitled this section (1:5-10):

II. The Platform for Fellowship (1:5-10)

He is giving us the condition, qualification, or platform upon which we must stand if we are going to have *fellowship* (partnership, doing business) with God. Now let's add the two sections contained within this "platform."

> II. The Platform for Fellowship (1:5-10)
>   A. Progression (1:5-7)
>   B. Proclamation of Sin (1:8-10)

Saturation on this progression through the day!

Day 8

Today we are going to begin to walk through the details of this first section (1:5-7). We must see this in light of the overall section. John is presenting the condition, qualification, or platform upon which we must stand if we are going to have *fellowship* (partnership, doing business) with God.

Let's saturate on the first verse of the section (1:5). Focus all day on its content. Notice how this verse ties you back to the introduction and at the same time introduces the expanded subject he wants to reveal. Write down all of the various ideas which you can see in the verse throughout the day.

Day 9

There is something about verse five which sets the tone for the entirety of this epistle. You see it clearly stated in **This is the message**. In this verse John is giving us some key details about this **message** before he even states what the actual content of the **message** is. Saturate on these details today.

You may want to get several translations of this verse and compare them to get a feel for the depth of the words involved. It is also helpful to write down the information as your think about it. This gives you the opportunity to go over it again and again.

1 John 1:5

Day 10

We want to take the information which developed from your saturation yesterday and expand it. This will help us receive the full impact of what John is saying in this opening statement.

In the original Greek text the sentence literally starts with the conjunction *And*. It is used in a larger sense than just a linkage between the introduction (1:1-4) and this opening statement. The introduction (1:1-4) becomes the threshold over which you are now going to walk into the large room. The room is actually going to be the *message*. It is not the *message* for this section but it is the whole room (the entire book). Each section of the book is going to be an investigation of the room.

Obviously the second word in the original Greek text is translated *this*. So the sentence begins *And this*. There is an emphasis established here which is very significance. This emphasis is going to be expanded in the words *which we have heard from Him*. All of this gives content to the *message*. *And this* states the impact of "there exists this as the message." Saturate on this idea today. Do not go over this lightly or dismiss it. It is a very significant idea. At the end of the day write a paragraph or page on the meaning of this concept.

1 John 1:5

Day 11

Let's go over the results of yesterday's saturation. There is a strong emphasis in the text that the *message* is bigger than our simple statement of it. It certainly exists apart from our declaration. We did not develop truth and formulate the *message*; rather the *message* was in existence and we are attempting to relate it. What we say about it will be inferior to the actual *message* itself.

Today saturate on some of the aspects of this concept to be sure they are comprehended:

> We are not the source of the *message*.

> We do not know the entirety of the *message* but are progressively learning.

> We did not discover the *message*; it discovered us

> The *message* was here before we were!

1 John 1:5

Day 12

Let's spend some time saturating on the idea of the *message*. Let me give you some insight into the Greek word translated *message*. It is a very unique word. It is only used twice as a noun in the New Testament. Both of the usages are in this epistle of 1 John (1:5; 3:11). It is only used one time in the New Testament as a verb (John 20:18). You can see that John is the only one who is highlighting this word.

He uses it in the sense of a promise! The word focuses on the content of that which is being proclaimed. In other words, the content of the *message* is supported or sourced by the sovereignty of God. There is a certainty about the *message*. If the **message** is from me, one might question its realty. If the *message* is from Satan, it is definitely a lie (John 8:44). The Greek word translated *message* has the idea of order or command.

With this as a background, saturate today on the idea of *message*. Make a list (from the passage – 1:5) of those items which give content to the message.

Day 13

Let's go over the list of concepts you discovered which give content to the *message*. One obvious concept of this *message* is that *which we have heard*. This gives definite content and establishes boundaries for the *message*. In the introduction the idea of hearing is expanded to include seeing and handling (1:1). All of these were a part of the hearing process. It is very significant that this verb is in the perfect tense. This describes something which happened in the past but has continuing results into the present.

The pronoun which is used is very exclusive. It is *we*. It relates back to those who were the eyewitnesses as described in the introduction (1:1-4). Saturate today on the affect the *message* had on them in the past and was even then continuing into the present. Can you not relate to this?

1 John 1:5

Day 14

We are looking at the list of concepts you discovered which give content to the *message*. One is the *message* was one *which we have heard*. Let's add the idea of *from Him*. The pronoun *Him* refers you back to the description given in the introduction (1:1-4). However is John referring to *His Son Jesus Christ* or to the *Father*?

It is very interesting that John uses a different Greek word in connection with the pronoun *Him*. In my translation it is correctly translated *from*. It is the only time he does this in any of his writings which makes it stand out. He normally would use the Greek word translated "of." Perhaps John is attempting to say something very pointedly to us. The primary meaning of this Greek word is *from*. It means the going forth or proceeding of one object from another. It indicates a separation of a person or an object from another person or an object with which it was formerly united. Therefore the phrase points to the ultimate and not necessarily the immediate source of the message. John may be the immediate source of the message, but he is not the ultimate source. Also *His Son Jesus Christ* may be the immediate source, but not the ultimate source.

Could John be referring to the *Father* as the ultimate source of the message? This would mean that the *message* came from the *Father* and became separate and distinct from Him. He is the ultimate source of it, but what John handled, heard, and saw was distinct from the *Father*. This is validated by his Gospel account (John 1:1-5). Saturate on this concept until you comprehend its depth.

1 John 1:5

Day 15

We have been saturating on the list of concepts you discovered (from the passage) which give content to the *message*. One is the idea of "Perceived." It is the *message* which has been distinctly delineated. It is so clear no one can misunderstand or misread it. Another is the fact of "Proceeding." We are not the source of the *message*. The ultimate source is the God, the Father.

We want to saturate today on the third concept. John states it as *and declare to you*. It is a translation of the Greek word "anangellein." It comes from the simple Greek verb "angellein." You will note the Greek word John uses is the simple Greek verb with a prefix. The prefix "ana" means "up to" or "back." Now this is contrasted with the Greek word "apangellein" which is used in verse three and also translated *declare*. It is the simple Greek verb with the prefix "apo" which is "from." You can see the emphasis in the declaration of the *message* is on John as simply an intermediary. He is an instrument of God for bringing "up to" the reader the revelation which has been separated from the Father and come to us.

There is an indication that the *message* is not simply stated or spoken, but lived. In other words it proceeded from the Father and was lived in the Son. Now it is coming from the Son and is living in us. This is the declaration! It is far beyond words. Yet, it is "Proclaimed."

1 John 1:5

Day 16

We are going to saturate today on the actual content of the *message*. Notice the two parts to the content of the *message*. There is the overwhelming statement: *God is light*. Next there is the statement: *in Him is no darkness at all.* It appears that the second statement gives clarification and content to the first statement. Let's saturate today on the fact that *God is light*.

Dwell on this thought all day long! Keep a card or paper close to jot down all thoughts about the aspect of *light*. Saturate this process in prayer.

1 John 1:5

Day 17

The danger of the process of yesterday's saturation is that outside of Divine revelation, we would simply consider the concept of *light* from our own cultural perspective. It must be clearly understood that the focus is on the very nature of God. This is not what He does or has, but what He is. This is a verb of "being." It is a statement of the absolute nature of God. He is not A *light*, nor is He THE *light*. In other words this statement is different than providing light as a function. He is not lighting our pathway (although He may do that). This is a focus on His nature.

Whenever there is a verb of "being," one must ask "Is there a subjective complement?" We discover there is by striking out the verb and replacing it with "equals." *God* equals *light*. It makes sense. Therefore, it is a subjective complement. This means you can reverse the sentence. *Light* equals *God*. They are the same. This is a focus on His nature.

In light of this statement, *God is light,* reflect on the statement *God is love* (1 John 4:8, 16). Both are expressing the nature of God; Who He is! How does *light* and *love* compare? Saturate today on their comparison. Keep notes on your thought throughout the day.

1 John 1:5

Day 18

Be sure in your saturation you are focusing on the nature of God. *God is light* is a direct statement about the nature of God. It is not about what He does or a function He performs. Do not over step the boundaries of the nature. Did you find some characteristics between *light* and *love*? You may want to take Paul's great statement about *love* (2 Corinthians 13) and see if the concept of *light* could be substituted. However, be sure and think only in terms of nature not activity. Continue in your saturation.

Day 19

Let's saturate on another aspect of the great *message*. **God is light** is not a metaphor. A metaphor is something with which you are familiar and it becomes a symbol of that with which you are not familiar. *It is a figure of speech in which a word or phrase that ordinarily designates one thing is used to designate another, thus making an implicit comparison* (dictionary). One great scholar stated: "All that we are accustomed to term 'light' in the domain of the creature, whether with a physical or metaphysical meaning, is only an effluence of that one and only primitive Light which appears in the nature of God" (Ebrard).

In the sentence, **God is light**, the word **light** is a predicate noun. This means it indicates quality. **Light** is the very being of God. It might be said, "God **lights**." God is **daylight**. There is only light in the presence of God. Saturate on the idea of God being **daylight**. Let this flood your life and mind. Make a list of your thoughts.

1 John 1:5

Day 20

It is important to see **God is light** through the eyes of the cultural environment in which John is writing. In the Hellenistic culture *light* was associated with excellence, purity, integrity, and wisdom. The contrast of *light-darkness* was parallel to that of heaven-earth, spirit-matter, higher-lower nature, true knowledge-false knowledge, and eternity-time. All of these contrasts were viewed as aspects of the basic opposition of the good and the bad principle. The adversaries of John were strongly influenced by these ideas. They wanted to enter the realm of light and escape the earthly realm along with its obligations. You can easily see this gave them the attitude of total indifference towards those who were not in the *light* as they were. John was giving new content to all of these contrasts. His view of *light-darkness* was an ethical one. It affected the very character of man. It changed the intentions and deeds of the individual. As we saturate in the rest of his epistle he will be constantly speaking to us about "love" toward our brother.

However, he is very strong on the reality that this is not a result of our nature but the nature of God who is *light*. We must have *fellowship* (koinonia) with God. Saturate on the interaction between you and the nature of God.

1 John 1:5

Day 21

The Greek language often uses one word for two concepts or two aspects of one concept. This is true with the Greek word for *light*. One great concept is the idea of "source" or "cause of." This is definitely the case in this verse (1:5) and also in the second chapter (2:8). If there is any *light* to be found it is because of God's nature. It is very important to understand that even the ungodly man experiences truth, love, and *light* because of the prevenient grace of God's presence. A second concept or aspect is the "effect" or "radiance" of the *light*. We see this as John begins to develop this theme (1:7; 2:9, 10). We will consider this in our saturation at another time.

Therefore, as you focus on the *light* limit your saturation to the concept of "source." It is used in this context to mean "clarity" or "brightness." It would be like "sunlight" or "daylight." In your saturation today focus on His personhood. There is nothing outside of His person. We are not seeking what He can do, but what He is. Our great need is to experience Him, and Him alone! Saturate in His presence!

1 John 1:5

Day 22

We would not be proper in our study if we did not consider the Old Testament. *Light* is constantly used as the express of the presence of God to His people. This expression was the first act of creation by this sovereign God (Genesis 1:3). He could not tolerate the darkness and void that had engulfed His world (Genesis 1:2). God led the Israelites with His presence through the wilderness. He was a "pillar of fire" (Exodus 13:21). He appeared and spoke to Moses in the wilderness *in a flame of fire from the midst of a bush* (Exodus 3:2). His descent upon Mt. Sinai was a great fire (Exodus 19:18).

It would be a good exercise to take your concordance and view this theme throughout the Old Testament. Saturate on the word *light*, fire, or lamp. This is the God who has become flesh and dwelt among us. This is the God we embrace and walk with in intimacy. Saturate on this wonder.

1 John 1:5

I want us to spend one more day focusing on the *light*. Perhaps you are familiar with the writing of Dante entitled "Paradise." It is certainly not in the same category as Scripture, but what a view he gives us. In the very opening he states:

> "The glory of Him who moveth everything
> Doth penetrate the universe, and shine
> In one part more and in another less.
> Within that heaven which most His light receives
> Was I."
> ("Paradiso," i., 1-5.)

Is this not the privilege which has been extended to you? *God is light*. This is the *message* lived before you and spoken to you. He Himself has come to bring this *light* (His nature). My grandboy in expressing his experience with God at the age of seven said, "It is like the *lights* came on!" Today in your saturation, consciously state this phrase *God is light* each moment an element of darkness approaches your life.

1 John 1:5

Day 24

We are going to begin our saturation on the additional phrase which gives content to the concept that *God is light* (1:5). It is the statement: *and in Him is no darkness at all.* This simple statement gives us a new dimension to the concept of *light*. John is establishing a contrast in order to give us a clear picture of the strength of the *light*.

This is not a new thing for him to do. Throughout his writings it is characteristic of John to express the same idea positively and negatively. We would do well to look at some of these in order to glean the impact he wants to make.

In your saturation today write down on a card the following verses and view them in light of the positive and negative contrast:

John 1:7, 8

John 3:15

John 3:17

1 John 1:6

1 John 1:7

1 John 2:4

1 John 5:12

Let's continue in our saturation *and in Him is no darkness at all.* It is really interesting to me the order of words as in the Greek text. It literally says, "And darkness there is not in Him, no, not in any way."

Do not assume you understand the content of *darkness*. *Darkness* is not a counterforce to the *light*. In other words John is not discussing two great forces in the universes. It is not a highlight of God and the Devil is combat. *Darkness* as John is using it is simply the absence of *light*. Anything which is not of the nature of God is viewed as *darkness*.

Saturate on this concept today. It is not about what would be considered good or bad, right or wrong, righteous or unrighteous. Anything not sourced by the nature of God is considered *darkness*. The only other great source for life's activities is the Devil. His nature is the carnal nature which is self-sovereignty. Anything sourced out of myself regardless of how good it may appear is *darkness*. In your saturation, examine all aspects of your living for the source.

1 John 1:5

Day 26

In our saturation of the great statement *and in Him is no darkness at all* we must not over look the significance of *in*. It is as if this is the entire key to the statement. It is all focused on what is taking place in and dominating the nature of God.

There are three little Greek words which might be looked at together in order to give us insight into what John is stating. Obviously he only used one of these words for his description of God. I am referring to "eis," "ek," and "en." The word used in our text (1:5) is "en." "En" stands between "eis" and "ek." "Eis" is the idea of into or unto which implies motion toward something or into something. "Ek" means out of or from which implies the motion of coming from something. But "en" is *in* meaning to remain in place.

In our text, John is not discussing what is emanating from God. It could be stated that *light* is shining from God to us, but this is not his intent in this verse. Certainly he is not wanting to tell us that *light* has come to God. Who is so great they could contribute to the nature of God? Rather he is discussing that which is permanently residing, constantly present, and always found in the nature of God. Again he is highlighting the idea of source. There is no *light* found outside of the nature of God. There is no chance of knowing *light* without intimacy with Him. I must find myself closer and closer to Him. This is worthy of your saturation today.

1 John 1:5

Day 27

We are again today going to saturate on the statement *and in Him is no darkness at all*. Contained within the statement is a double negative. There is the Greek word which is translated *no*. It literally means "not." But John was not satisfied with saying this once. He added the Greek word which is translated *at all*. This Greek word is a compound word. It is the Greek word translated "not" and "one" combined. The author is being very definite about this statement. This compound word generally means "no one," "nothing," or "none at all." It particularly places the emphasis on "not even one" or "not the least."

It would be good to saturate today on the use of this word keeping in mind the double negative. For instance, John is consistently using this word concerning Jesus. He highlights the exclusivity of who He is! Consider these Scriptures:

John 3:2 – "No one can do these signs."

John 3:13 – "No one has ascended into heaven."

John 5:19 – "The Son can do nothing by Himself."

John 6:44, 65 – "No one can come to me."

John 7:27 – "When the Messiah comes, no one will know."

John 11:49 – "Only the Son knows: 'You know nothing'."

John 14:6 – "No one comes to the Father except through me."

1 John 1:5

Day 28

Light is immaterial, diffusive, pure, and glorious. It is the condition of life. Physically, it represents glory; intellectually, truth; morally, holiness. As immaterial it corresponds to God as spirit; as diffusive, to God as love; as the condition of life, to God as life; as pure and illuminating, to God as holiness and truth. (Taken from Vincent's Word Studies in the New Testament.)

If this is true then:

> God is Spirit
>
> God is love
>
> God is life
>
> God is holy
>
> God is truth.

Anything outside of this nature is *darkness*. I do not want anything but Him. Again today saturate on Him. Embrace Him. Allow nothing to distract you from Him. The sum total of your need is for Him. Focus on Him!

1 John 1:5

Verse five has been a powerful verse to investigate. Having investigated the various aspects of the verse, we need to return to the over all meaning. Let's review so we can see verse five in proper perspective. The entire purpose of the writing is about *fellowship* (see verse 3). However it is not fellowship in just having a good time, but is intimately connected to "doing business." It is joining God in the great enterprise of His heart. The Greek word is "koinonia." Everything in verse five through ten of this chapter is calling us into *fellowship*.

These verses more specifically give us the "Platform for *Fellowship*." He begins this discussion with the "Progression" (1:5-7). The focus of these verses is the idea of *walk*. As he moves into this idea he presents the "Protocol" (1:5). This is the great and overwhelming *message*. It is the basis of it all. This is the foundation for all *fellowship*. It is the fact that *God is light and in Him is no darkness at all.* We are being called upon to *walk* with this God. Is this not saturation in His very presence? Again today develop the pattern of being aware of His nature within you. Let His light permeate every aspect of your activities. Bring every speck of *darkness* into His *light*.

1 John 1:5

Day 30

Let's go back to our outline in order to help us keep things in perspective.

    I. Introduction (1:1-4)
        A. The Person (1:1, 2)
            1. Past to the Present (1:1a)
            2. Physical Testimony (1:1b)
            3. Proclamation (1:2)
        B. The Purpose (1:3, 4)
            1. (of the) Proclamation (1:3)
                a. Partnership with us (1:3)
                b. Partnership with Father (1:3)
                c. Partnership with His Son (1:3)
            2. (of the) Printing (1:4)
                a. Pepleerooménee (1:4)
                b. Pleasurable Contentment (1:4)

    II. The Platform for Fellowship (1:5-10)
        C. Progression (1:5-7)
            1. Protocol
                a. Perceived (1:5)
                b. Proceeding (1:5)
                c. Proclaimed (1:5)

Be sure you understand the progression of the outline. The purpose is to give you key words which highlight the truth in which you have saturated. You may need to go back over the past days and review the material. John begins the call to *walk* with the *message*. The *message* is "perceived." It became flesh and lived among us. It was "proceeding" *from Him* (1:5). We certainly are not the source of the *message*. Now John has "proclaimed" the *message* to us that *God is light and in Him is no darkness at all*. Again today saturate in the reality of this truth.

Word

from

Word

Part Four
1 John 1:6

Day 1

We have just finished verse five of the first chapter of this great book. We have discovered the purpose of the entire writing is that we might have *fellowship* (partnership) with Him (1:3). Everything we study must be interpreted in light of this purpose. We are looking carefully at the section called "The Platform for Fellowship (1:5-10)." This section completes the first chapter. John begins his discussion of *fellowship* by linking it with the idea of a *walk* (1:6, 7). This paints the picture of a progression (something on the move). The first step in this progression was the "Protocol (1:5)." It is the understanding that *God is light and in Him is no darkness at all*. Now we are ready to move into verse six.

In your saturation today write verse six and verse seven on a card to carry with you. All day long write notes of the contrast you see between the two. Note as many aspects of the contrast between *light* and *darkness* (as distinguished in these verses) as you can.

1 John 1:6

Day 2

Having saturated in the contrast between verse six and seven (*light* and *darkness*), let's begin our saturation in verse six.

It is very important at this point to understand the cultural setting and environment to which John is writing. It is certainly not unlike our own condition. In fact this situation has been in every generation throughout Church history. It is best described in the word "antinomianism." This term comes from the Greek word "anti" which means "against" and "nomos" which means "law." At first glance this may seem to appear to be exactly what Paul proposed in his epistles. We are delivered from the law and are living in the grace of God supplied by the death of Christ. However, antinomianism takes this great truth and carries it beyond what Paul was proposing. If Christ delivered us from the law, then we are under no obligation to obey even the moral laws of God. We are free to live in grace as we live in acts of disobedience and sin. Grace means it simply does not matter how we live.

John is going to bombard this false teaching with consistent truth in this epistle. He will not tolerate this idea for one moment. In light of this, saturate again in verse six. Through prayer begin a careful examination of your own attitude concerning antinomianism.

1 John 1:6

Day 3

Again let's take note of the great proposition which is being given to us in verse five. **God is light and in Him is no darkness at all** (1:5). If **God is light** to the very exclusion of all **darkness**, then *fellowship* (partnership) with **darkness** would absolutely exclude any *fellowship with Him*.

It is absolutely necessary that you saturation on this great proposition until it is a part of your very thinking. If there is any misunderstanding of this idea you will have strong arguments with the writings of the rest of this book and especially the next two verses. This issue must be settled in your mind and heart.

In your saturation be careful not to allow your own living to justify questioning the basic proposition. This proposition must not be considered false because your life style indicates it. This would mean that our experiences and life styles determine what is true about God. We must let our life experiences be determined by truth about God; not the truth about God to be determined by our life experiences.

Saturate in honesty today!

1 John 1:6

Day 4

Let me restate the great proposition from yesterday's saturation. You should be able to quote it from memory. *God is light and in Him is no darkness at all* (1:5). If *God is light* to the very exclusion of all *darkness*, then *fellowship* (partnership) with *darkness* would absolutely exclude any *fellowship with Him*.

We are now entering into verse six based upon this great proposition. Notice the beginning word of the sentence is *If*. In this verse this word is a conjunction formed by the combination of two Greek words. The first Greek word is "ei." It is conditional particle which means *If*. However, there is a second word combined with it which is "an." This is a particle which focuses on supposition, wish, possibility, or uncertainty. Thus, the word beginning our sentence is "Ean."

When "ei" (merely "if") is used it expresses a condition which is hypothetical or a subjective possibility. However when it is combined with "an" as in our verse it implies a condition which must be determined by experience, an objective possibility. It always refers to something in the future. It is usually connected or followed by the subjunctive as in our verse. *We say* is in the subjunctive mood.

You need to clearly understand this! The force of the statement then is not conditional or hypothetical. The author is not saying, "If we say we have fellowship with Him, then we walk in darkness." The act of stating we have fellowship with God is not the cause of us being in darkness. This is not a conditional statement. Rather, the *If* is expectational. This means it introduces something which under certain present circumstances is expected to occur. It has the idea of "when" or "whenever." In other words, WE LIE, WHENEVER we say that we have fellowship with God, and yet walk in darkness.

Again John is stating there is no possibility of having fellowship with God and linking with darkness. If God is light to the very exclusion of all darkness, then fellowship (partnership) with darkness would absolutely exclude any fellowship with Him. I realize this is very narrow, but is it true. Saturate on its truth today until you at least understand it, even if you don't accept it!

1 John 1:6

Day 5

Today we want to saturate on the phrase *we say*. There is a great lesson to be learned by John's approach. We realize he is an old man by this time. He is referring to those to whom he is writing as *My little children* (2:1), *Beloved* (3:21; 4:1, 7, 11). This is not one who is scolding or accusing. In fact, notice in the phrase in which we are saturating today, he included himself. The falsehood he is addressing is antinomianism. No doubt some of the individuals of the church have been influenced by this fallacy.

However, in a very tactful way, he is bringing truth to them. I have noticed in the fellowship of the church, we seldom use this approach. We speak in a "you" or "them" language. It is as if we need no correction or stand above the need of examination. John is willing to place himself in the same category he is placing them. They lie, whenever they say they have fellowship with God and walk in darkness. The same is true for John. Thus, he uses the pronoun *we*.

Carefully examine your approach to others in your church. Is it "them" or "us?" In your prayers at church are you praying for God to speak to them or to us? Are you exempt of needing to hear the voice of God? Are you willing to experience the same examinations you are calling "them" to take? Let this be a day of application.

1 John 1:6

We are continuing in our saturation of the phrase *we say*. This verb is in the subjunctive mood. It works hand in hand with *If* at the beginning of the verse. It suggests an action or a state which is contingent, probable, or eventual. In other words, this action or state may not occur in the future, but it is inevitable if the circumstances are right. What are the circumstances and what is the state or action? He is speaking of "lying and not practicing the truth." This state will take place if the circumstance is right. Again what is the circumstance which produces this state? It is acknowledging that we are in partnership with Him in the great enterprise of His heart *(fellowship)* and *walking in darkness*.

Be sure and saturate to the point of complete comprehension and even memorization. *God is light and in Him is no darkness at all* (1:5). If *God is light* to the very exclusion of all *darkness*, then *fellowship* (partnership) with *darkness* would absolutely exclude any *fellowship with Him*.

1 John 1:6

Day 7

If we say we have fellowship with Him, is the focus of our saturation today. Let's go back and review the key word, *fellowship.* It is the Greek word "koinonian." You may want to go back into the previous saturation studies and review the details concerning this word. It has the primary meaning of joint-participation with someone else in things possessed in common by both individuals. It was originally focused on the idea of business or an enterprise. The business venture was the common element bringing the individuals together. This is certainly true with our *fellowship* with God. However the joint-participation in common elements between us and God is the common nature we now experience. This gives us common likes and dislikes. From the common nature a communion of interest and activities which we call *fellowship* take place. One American Indian language translates this word *fellowship* as "God and I are of one mind."

If we are of the same mind, common nature, with God, what is His nature? This is the "protocol." **God is light and in Him is no darkness at all** (1:5). If **God is light** to the very exclusion of all *darkness*, then *fellowship* (partnership) with *darkness* would absolutely exclude any *fellowship with Him*. It is an absolute impossibility! Thoroughly saturate on this concept today.

1 John 1:6

Before we investigate the meaning of the words in the next phrase, *and walk in darkness,* we need to stand back and view the connection of the phrase with the entire verse. This statement is the second part of the sentence which is governed by the conjunction *if.* Remember, the conjunction *if* is really the idea of "when."

This second part of the sentence, *and walk in darkness,* is in strong contrast to the first part, *If we say that we have fellowship with Him.* There seem to be two strong contrasts:

we say | we walk

fellowship with Him | in darkness

Saturate on these two contrasts today. Perhaps you will want to write a list of comparisons between these ideas.

1 John 1:6

Day 9

In light of saturation from yesterday, let's highlight the word *and* which introduces this second statement in the contrast. It is the Greek word "kai." It is a primary particle which has a copulative and often a cumulative affect. In this sentence, this word has an adversative force or opposing force. In this sentence, it could easily be translated "and yet," "but," or "but at the same time." It might read "and yet it is *in darkness* that we *walk*" or "but our life has only *darkness*."

You can easily see the strong contrast of extreme opposites being presented by John. *Fellowship with Him* would mean *light*. So the extreme contrast is *light* and *darkness*. Let this extreme contrast be your saturation for today. On the one hand is *fellowship* (partnership with common interest, nature) *with Him*. On the other hand is *darkness*. On the one hand is talking about *fellowship with Him*. On the other hand is the actual *walk in darkness*. Don't allow this to just be an exercise or concept. Spend time applying this to your life.

1 John 1:6

Day 10

Today our saturation will focus on the concept of *walk*. This is a translation from the Greek word "peripateo." The basic word "pateo" means to walk. So our word in the text has the prefix "peri" on it. This has the idea of "around."

Notice how the word is used in these following verses:

> 1 Peter 5:8
> Galatians 5:16
> 1 Thessalonians 2:12
> Ephesians 4:1
> Ephesians 5:8
> Colossians 1:10

Would you not agree that each time in the context of the usage of the word activity is demonstrated? The focus of the word is on movement. The focus of his intent is not on inactivity. In other words, he is not discussing what you do not do or the bad things in which you do not participate. This is not a list of negative and positive rules. This is the general activity of life. Perhaps better stated, it is the atmosphere, bent, or force involved in all of the activities of life.

Take these additional verses above with you throughout the day. Saturate on the context of the word *walk*.

1 John 1:6

Day 11

From yesterday's saturation you have gleaned a feel for the action of the word translated *walk*. John is definitely referring to our daily life, our movement and activity in this world. This seems to be the key to this verse. It is this *walk* which is the expression to the *fellowship* (koinonia) in which we live. Again we are face to face with only two options. On the one hand there is *fellowship with Him*. On the other hand there is *walk in darkness*. It is the *walk* which determines your partnership not what you say.

Remember John was confronting the falsehood of antinomianism (see Day Two). Some were beginning to believe they were the enlightened. To this group all action was indifferent. It simply did not matter. Neither purity nor filth can change the nature of pure gold; therefore the inner spirit in all that matters. We are not affected by the activities of the flesh. But John is shouting you have become false in both word (*we say*) and in deed (*walk in darkness*).

Let your saturation today be in the application of this great truth. Be honest!

1 John 1:6

Day 12

Today in our saturation we are confronted with the concept of *darkness* again. You may need to go back to last month's saturation and review. Anything which is not Jesus is *darkness*. If *God is light* anything outside of Him is in the realm of *darkness* regardless of how right it may appear.

This noun is in the dative case. In this verse (1 John 1:6) it is a locative dative. This means that *darkness* indicates the place in which the verb's action occurs. In other words the one who *walks in darkness* conducts himself in the sphere of sin. Nothing of the *light* of God is involved in his *walk*. John is going to move from the use of the word *darkness* in this verse to the word *sin* in the next verse. Throughout this epistle he will interchange these two words.

It is as if there is a two fold aspect to this *darkness*. We will begin to see this clearly as we saturate in the following sections of the book. There is definitely the deed or action of sin, but also this sphere or nature in which the deed is promoted. *God is light* is far beyond deeds that God does. It is the very nature and sphere in which God dwells. So it is with the *walk in darkness*. It is not a matter of doing a deed once and then not doing it again for another month. It is a matter of the sphere or source of the very action or movement of your life.

Carefully search your own heart (not is a quick moment, but in saturation).

1 John 1:6

Day 13

We want to be sure to have comprehended the idea of *darkness* as expressed in our verse. Remember this noun is a locative dative. This means that *darkness* indicates the place in which the verb's action occurs. If we are not people of the *light* then we are *walking in darkness*. It is far greater than just some deeds which through discipline can be eliminated. This is a nature or attitude that is the motivating and driving force of your life. We are again dealing with the issue of source.

It may help us to saturate on this word *darkness* as used in the New Testament. Write John 3:19 on a card and saturate in its content. Note the contrast between *light* and *darkness*. Notice also the distinction between the evil deeds and the sphere of *darkness*.

1 John 1:6

Day 14

Let's continue our saturation on the concept of *darkness*. There are certainly the activities of *darkness* but the very nature and sphere of *darkness* is the real source of concern. In describing what God, the Father, has done in redeeming the world, we get a vivid picture of the incarnation from the Apostle Paul.

Carefully view 2 Corinthians 4:6.

Write it on a card and saturate on its meaning throughout the day. Especially notice the following items:

> The Source of the Light - God
>
> The Son of the Light – Jesus Christ
>
> The Sphere of the Light – Treasure (verse 7)
>
> The Shining of the Light – In our hearts
>
> The Surroundings of the Light – Darkness

1 John 1:6

Day 15

We want to continue with our saturation on the concept of *darkness*. We have been viewing some of the other great passages in the Scriptures which give us content to this concept. We are attempting to take this content and bring it into our passage in 1 John.

In 2 Corinthians 6:14, we have additional information which is vital to our understanding. Remember the basic "Protocol" which is the context of our verse in 1 John 1:6. *God is light and in Him is no darkness at all* (1:5). If *God is light* to the very exclusion of all *darkness*, then *fellowship* (partnership) with *darkness* would absolutely exclude any *fellowship with Him*.

Saturate in 2 Corinthians 6:14 and view how the Apostle Paul states this same concept in a practical application to our own lives. Notice the following in your saturation throughout the day:

There are three contrasts –
> Equally Yoked – Unequally Yoked
> Righteousness – Lawlessness
> *Light – Darkness*

As he continues into the following verses, he extends the contrasts:
> Christ – Belial
> Believer – Unbeliever
> Temple – Idols

All of this is an expression of being filled with the Holy Spirit. We are to be filled with the *Light* that God is!

1 John 1:6

Day 16

We do not want to belabor the issue of *light* and *darkness*, but it is such an important concept for the book of 1 John and our lives. Let's continue to saturate on it today.

Look at the Scripture found in 1 Thessalonians 5:5. Do I need to remind you to write this down on a card so you can saturate on it throughout the day? This also gives you the opportunity to write notes on the back of the card. It is a key verse, but you need to see the context of it in 1 Thessalonians. Paul actually begins in verse four and continues into verse seven speaking concerning the *light* and *darkness*.

Notice the following subjects within the context of *darkness*:

      Separated (there are only two categories)

      Seeing (we are alert – see verse two)

      Sons (we have His nature)

      Sleeping (we are awake because of *light*)

      Sober (we are sober because of *light*)

1 John 1:6

Day 17

There is one last verse which we absolutely have to include in our saturation on the subject of *light* and *darkness*. It is 1 Peter 2:9. You will again need to write it on a card and allow it to penetrate your life throughout this day.

Rejoice in the description of who you are in Him! Notice the climax of the verse is you are *called . . . out of darkness into His marvelous light*. What is the content of this position or calling?

> Chosen Generation
>
> Royal Priesthood
>
> Holy Nation
>
> His own Special People

What is the purpose of the calling?

> People of the *Light*

Day 18

It would be proper for your saturation today to be a review. I would like for you to take all of the verses we have considered and see how they give content to 1 John 1:6. This should be easy to do, since you have a card with the verse and additional notes recording your saturation.

The verses we considered are: John 3:19; 2 Corinthians 4:6; 6:14; 1 Thessalonians 5:5; 1 Peter 2:9.   This process should give you a broader view of the concept of our verse.

1 John 1:6

Day 19

As you begin your saturation today, make a new card for 1 John 1:6. It is important to stand back and look at the entirety of the verse. As you study the parts of the verse, you need to keep them in the context of the entire verse. This is really important. Don't become so enamored with the trees you miss the view of the forest.

Notice the structure of the sentence. There are two basic parts to this sentence. The first part is a positive statement; the second part is a negative. Stating that *we have fellowship with Him* is a very positive thing to do. However, *walking in darkness, we lie and do not practice the truth* is very negative. This structure seems to be very important to John. Notice he does this a number of times in the verses which immediately follow (see verse 8 and verse 10).

This contrast is important for it appears these are the only two categories available. You are either in one or the other. Don't be fooled by a third option. Notice the additional contrast between these statements:

> Positive – Negative
> *Light – Darkness*
> Partnership with Him – Partnership with Satan
> Practicing Truth – Not Practicing Truth
> Truth – Lies

Saturate on these contrasts throughout the day.

We have become aware of the structure of 1 John 1:6. There is a positive statement and a negative statement. We have already saturated on the positive statement. What a staggering possibility to become partners (koinonia) with God.

As you saturate today on the negative statement in this verse, notice it is divided into three sections. We have actually already spent some time on the first of the three statements. Each statement is an attempt to restate and give content the other two statements. Or you may consider the proposition of the negative statement is *walk in darkness* and *we lie and do not practice the truth* is a restatement. When John completes these three statements, there is no question about what the opposite of walking in the light is!

Saturate on these three statements and make notes on how they contribute to each other.

1 John 1:6

Day 21

Since we have spent some time in saturating on the phrase *walk in darkness*, you will only need to review its meaning and application. Now we want to saturate on *we lie*. Obviously John is saying that when we live our life according to the pattern of the sphere of darkness, *we lie* if we claim any contact with *light*.

In your saturation on this phrase, it is important to understand that in the writings of John the Greek word translated *we lie* refers to all that is not of God. In other words, it is the very opposite of *God is light*. This includes not only words but also attitudes and actions. See how strong John is as he describes the condition in a person's life who is attempting to appear to have *fellowship with Him* and yet is *walk*ing *in darkness*. Such a person is a *liar* (1 John 2:4). There is definitely a focus on the falsehood of words, since the sentence begins with *If we say*. However, this falsehood spreads to attitudes and actions as well. You see this clearly in the last phrase *do not practice the truth*.

Saturate on the concept that anything which is not in the *Light* is a *lie*. Anything not sourced by the Spirit of Jesus in your life, regardless of how good, is a *lie*. When we are sourced in our business out of the patterns of the world, we base our business on a *lie*. If not sourced by God, our marriage is based on a *lie*. Let this grip you today through saturation.

1 John 1:6

Day 22

In light of our passage, let's saturate in two other verses to verify we are on the right track. Take a card and write down Hebrews 6:18 and Titus 1:2. Saturate on these two verses today. There is an understanding in the New Testament that since *God is light*, it is absolutely impossible for Him to *lie*. Notice both of the above verses focus on the promises of God. They have to do with an oath.

As we apply this truth to our verse (1 John 1:6), we want to see the utter impossibility of having *fellowship with Him* and to *walk in darkness*. It is a falsehood. We have once again verified the basic premise or "Protocol." *God is light and in Him is no darkness at all* (1:5). If *God is light* to the very exclusion of all *darkness*, then *fellowship* (partnership) with *darkness* would absolutely exclude any *fellowship with Him*.

Day 23

We need to saturate on one other aspect of this statement, *we lie*. It is highlighted for us in the Gospel of John (8:44). Write this verse down on a card and write notes on it as you see it in light of our verse (1 John 1:6).

Notice the *lie* has a personal representative who also produces children. *God is light* (truth) also has a personal representative who also produces children. In your saturation be sure and note the context. It is the most righteous people of Jesus' day that Jesus is addressing.

Consider the following contrasts in your saturation:

Source – God (truth) or Devil (lie)

Standing – in truth or in a lie

Speaking – always truth or always a lie

Seeking – God who is light or *his own resources*

Start – In the beginning God (*is light*) or *murder from the beginning*

Sire – Children of *light* or children of a *lie*

1 John 1:6

Day 24

The most dramatic place in the New Testament highlighting the demonic nature of lying is found in the Book of Acts chapter five. It is the story of Ananias and Sapphira. Everyone in the early church was selling all they had and bringing it into the church for the use of the Kingdom (Acts 4:34). This couple did not want to be left out. They also *sold a possession* (Acts 5:1) and brought the money to the apostles. However, they only brought part of the proceeds. But this was not the issue. They lied about bringing all. They did not survive the condition of lying for both of them died. On a card copy two verses (Acts 5:3, 4). Write notes on these verses and the story for your saturation today. Notice the following issues:

Source of the Lie – Satan (Acts 5:3)

Surrender of the Lie – Partial (Acts 5:3)

Seat of the Lie – Heart (Acts 5:3, 4)

Scheme of the Lie – Against the Holy Spirit (Acts 5:3, 4)

Style of the Lie – Self-style (Acts 5:3)

State of the Lie – Death (Acts 5:5)

Sway of the Lie – (Acts 5:1)

1 John 1:6

Day 25

We are going to begin saturating on the last phrase of verse six. Remember the verse is divided into a positive statement and then a negative statement. The positive statement is a focus on *fellowship* (koinonia) *with Him*. The opposite or negative is to *walk in darkness, we lie and do not practice the truth*. This great truth must be seen in light of the "Protocol." *God is light and in Him is no darkness at all* (1:5). If *God is light* to the very exclusion of all *darkness*, then *fellowship* (partnership) with *darkness* would absolutely exclude any *fellowship with Him*.

The major statement is *walk in darkness*. This is explained or has content. *We lie* is given as the exposed heart of *walking in darkness*. However, further explanation is given by stating *do not practice the truth*. Let's begin our saturation on this last phrase.

A literal translation from the original language would be "we do not do the truth." Write this phrase on a card and make notes on it as you saturate on this concept. Take into consideration what is means "to do." What is the truth?

1 John 1:6

As we continue saturating on the phrase *and do not practice the truth*, be aware of this same construction in other parts of this epistle. Often John gives the verb *to do* and then follows it by an abstract noun. Take note of the following verses:

To do the will of God (1 John 2:17)

To do righteousness (1 John 2:29; 3:7, 10)

To do sin (1 John 3:4, 8)

To do lawlessness (1 John 3:4)

To do what is pleasing before Him (1 John 3:22)

To do His commandments (1 John 5:2)

While your translation may not read *do*, in each case it is a translation of the same Greek word as used in our text (1 John 1:6). View each of these verses and saturate on *to do*. What does it mean *to do*?

1 John 1:6

Day 27

Today we want to saturate on the actual Greek word translated *do*. This particular Greek word is highlighted in John's Gospel and epistles. It is the Greek word "poieo." This Greek word is best understood when contrasted with another Greek word translated *do*. It is the Greek word "prasso." The best illustration of their usages is in the Gospel of John (5:29). There are two groups who are going to come forth from the graves. There are *those who have done* (poieo) *good* and *those who have done* (prasso) *evil*.

"Poieo" literally means to create. It paints the picture of a tree that "does" fruit. There is something inside the tree which flows in creativity and the result is fruit. It is not strained but natural and normal. It is the picture of the artist who is painting a masterpiece on canvas. There is a creativity flowing through the artist which guides the strokes of the brush.

"Prasso" gives the picture of duty, habit, or routine. It is the picture of the barn painter who is getting paid by the hour. He is not an artist, but fulfilling his obligation in order to be paid.

We are a people who have become partners (koinonia) with God. We are in intimate *fellowship with Him*. The creative flow of the Holy Spirit is producing His fruit through us. We certainly are participating, but it is His life through us which is *doing*. Take this concept and bring it into our verse. If one is actually *walk*ing *in darkness*, there is nothing of the creative flow of the Holy Spirit through him. It is actually impossible for him to *do* (poieo) *truth*. He may be able to *do* (prasso) rules and religious observances. In other words, the only way *light* can be seen in and through him is for the One who is *light* to produce it through him. This is giving us a strengthened content to the idea of *fellowship* (koinonia).

Saturate on the difference between "poieo" and "prasso." See it in the context of the *lie* in our verse.

1 John 1:6

Day 28

Our saturation today must focus on the word *truth*. We must take what we learned yesterday concerning *to do* (poieo) and apply it to *truth*.

In a private conversation between Pilate and Jesus during the trial, *Pilate said to Him, "What is truth?"* (John18:38). It is an age old question and yet fresh on our lips in this study. This question has been stimulated by a previous statement Jesus had made. *Jesus answered, "You say rightly that I am a king. For this cause I was born, and for this cause I have come into the world, that I should bear witness to the truth. Everyone who is of the truth hears My voice,"* (John 18:37).

In speaking to His disciple, *Jesus said to him, "I am the way, the truth, and the life,"* (John 14:6). One begins to sense the *truth* as He speaks of it is far above facts, data, or information. It has to do with authenticity, Divine reality, and revelation. What happened to man in the "fall" brought him to a position of the *lie*. There was no creative flow of the Spirit to bring about an embracing of the *truth*. Man could *do* (prasso) the *truth*, but he could not *do* (poieo) the *truth*. It is in embracing the *truth* (Jesus) that one is enabled to *do* (poieo) the *truth*.

Saturate on this concept today!

1 John 1:6

Let's take what we have learned from the last few days and place it in the context of our verse (1 John 1:6). Walking in *fellowship* (koinonia) *with Him* and *walk*ing *in darkness* are mutually exclusive. There can be no mixing of the two. If someone states they are in partnership (koinonia) with God, while they are *walk*ing *in darkness,* it is a *lie.* *Darkness* is not just an activity, but is a sphere in which one lives. It is anything which is not of Jesus. A *lie* must be seen as anything which is outside of Christ. Therefore the content of *darkness* is a *lie.* The content of a *lie* is *and do not practice the truth.* In order to *do* (poieo) the *truth,* the One who is the *truth* must reside within and enable the responding individual. *Truth* is completely beyond activities or intellectual acceptance. *Truth* is expressions of the very life of God bringing revelation of His life. As Jesus was the *truth* because of the creative flow of the Father within and through Him, so we are the *truth* because of the creative flow of Jesus within and through us. This flow and expression of *truth* is summarized in *light.* You are in one or the other.

Saturate today in this summary. Let this verse grip your heart and change your life!

1 John 1:6

Day 30

It is our purpose today to complete 1 John 1:6 by placing it into the outline of the great epistle which we have been developing. Remember the purpose of an outline is to remind us of the concepts and truths which we have grasp. This helps us to see where the author has come from and where he is going to.

Review the first part of the outline which established the purpose for the entire book. Everything must be understood in light of this purpose. This will determine the interpretation of every verse.

    I. Introduction (1:1-4)
        A. The Person (1:1, 2)
            1. Past to the Present (1:1a)
            2. Physical Testimony (1:1b)
            3. Proclamation (1:2)
        B. The Purpose (1:3, 4)
            1. (of the) Proclamation (1:3)
                a. Partnership with us (1:3)
                b. Partnership with Father (1:3)
                c. Partnership with His Son (1:3)
            2. (of the) Printing (1:4)
                a. Pepleerooménee (1:4)
                b. Pleasurable Contentment (1:4)

Now we must move to the next section which goes from verse five to the end of the chapter, verse ten. It is

    II. The Platform for Fellowship (1:5-10)
        D. Progression (1:5-7)
            1. Protocol

      a. Perceived (1:5)

      b. Proceeding (1:5)

      c. Proclaimed (1:5)

2. Pattern of Darkness (1:6)

There are four basic ideas which we have discovered in our saturation in this verse (1 John 1:6). You will want to add to the outline by stating these ideas. I will give you a suggestion concerning words to use, but you may choose your own.

2. Pattern of Darkness (1:6)

      a. Presumption (1:6)

      b. Peripateo (walk) (1:6)

      c. Pseudometha (lie) (1:6)

      d. Poieo (do) (1:6)

In your saturation today, review these words and let the content of this verse be cemented into your life!

Word *from* Word

Part Five
1 John 1:7

1 John 1:7

Day 1

We are beginning our investigation of verse seven of chapter one. It contains some tremendous insight for us. It is especially focused on the issue of victory over all darkness. As we begin we must rediscover the purpose or theme of the entire book of 1 John. It is *fellowship* (1:3). Remember this is not "pot-luck supper" fellowship, but koinonia. It has to do with "doing business" or "partnership."

In your saturation today concentrate on the first seven verses. Look at these verses through the eyes of *fellowship* (partnership). See the number of times this word is stated. Who is involved in this *fellowship* each time?

The author states the word *fellowship* two times in verse three. Each time it is focused on a different recipient. Now in verse six and seven he does the same thing. Is this coincidence?

1 John 1:7

Day 2

Now that you have in mind the flow of verse one through seven and the parallel of the *fellowship* (partnership) of verse three with verses six and seven, we can begin our investigation of verse seven. There is a distinct connection between verses six and seven which must be recognized. It is a contrast!

Verse seven begins with the contrasting conjunction **But**. The primary function of this word is to establish contrasting pictures. Therefore verse six gives us one side of the picture, while verse seven now presents the contrasting side.

Take a card and write on it these two verses. On the back side begin to list the contrasts suggested between the two verses. It will give you a clear picture of the content of verse seven.

1 John 1:7

Day 3

We need to spend another day saturating on the list of contrasts from yesterday. Perhaps our focus today should be in applying these contrasts to our own lives. Look closely at the list again. Does it include the following?

1. Walking in darkness (1:6) – Walking in light (1:7)
2. If we say (1:6) – If we walk (actually) (1:7)
3. Fellowship with Him (1:6) – Fellowship with one another (1:7)
4. Do not practice the truth (1:6) – Cleanses us from all sin (1:7)
5. We lie (1:7) – The blood of Jesus Christ His Son (1:7)
6. Lie (1:6) – Truth (1:7)
7. No "poieo" (do) (1:6) – Blood is cleansing (1:7)
8. We say (self sourcing) (1:6) – As He is (Light sourcing) (1:7)

1 John 1:7

Day 4

In our outline you will notice we have listed verse six as "The Pattern of Darkness." I want to suggest to you we list verse seven as "The Pattern of Light." Let's review the outline to cement this in our minds.

II. The Platform for Fellowship (1:5-10)
   A. Progression (1:5-7)
      1. Protocol
      2. Pattern of Darkness (1:6)
      3. Pattern of Light (1:7)

Verses one through four present to us the introduction to the book which tells us the theme and purpose of the writing. As we have already discovered it has to do with *fellowship* (partnership). Now we are considering the "Progression" of this *fellowship.* This is suggested to us through the idea of *walk* which is stated in both verses six and seven in the contrast. We will look closely at this idea as we begin to deal with the specific words of verse seven.

In your saturation today, look at the opposing patterns. See your activities, expressions, and attitudes as a part of one of these patterns. In which pattern are you walking - in *darkness* or in *light*?

1 John 1:7

Day 5

Yesterday you were to view your activities, motives, and attitudes in one category or the other of the contrast. It is a contrast between the "Pattern of darkness" (1:6) and the "Pattern of light" (1:7). Perhaps you had some difficulty in placing each activity. After all, there are many normal activities of life which are in everyone's life. This would be true of the people of darkness and people of light. These activities do not have anything to do with the spiritual realm. It is simply who we are as a part of humanity.

While this seems logical, it is not Biblical! In the passage at hand and throughout the rest of this epistle we are discovering only two realms, *light* and *darkness*. There is not a third category. Each activity of life is of *light* or *darkness* due to your personal linkage, fellowship, koinonia. You must be in business (fellowship) with one or the other. If you are not sourced by the *light*, then *darkness* is automatic. So spend another day saturating in verse seven. Are you sourced by the *light*?

Day 6

John introduces our statement in verse seven with the little word *if.* It is the Greek word "ean." You will notice that verses six, seven, eight, nine, and ten all begin with this same word. It is not being used in the same way each time. Verses six, eight, and ten have a different usage than verses seven and nine. You may need to go back to "Day Four" in volume four of our series and study that material again.

The difference is not in the actual word "ean," but is the verb to which it is connected. In verses six, eight, and ten the main verb is in the aorist subjunctive while in verses seven and nine it is the present subjunctive.

This presents us with a different view between verse six and seven. In verse six, the force of *if* is "expectational." It introduces something which under certain circumstances and from a given standpoint is expected to occur. It presents the idea of "when." In other words, when we walk in darkness and say we have fellowship (partnership) with God, WE LIE.

Now in verse seven *if* is used in the "conditional" sense. The necessary condition is *walk in the light.* If this is the reality condition of our life, then it results in *fellowship with one another, and the blood of Jesus Christ His Son cleanses us from all sin.*

Do you see the difference between the two? In the first you could *walk in darkness* and not lie. "Walking in darkness" does not mean you will say you have fellowship with Him. Obviously one could *walk in darkness* and admit they do not have fellowship with God. Therefore "walking in darkness" does not necessarily produce this lie. However, in verse seven to *walk in the light* is a condition which automatically produces two things. It produces *fellowship with one another* and *the blood of Jesus Christ His Son cleanses us from all sin.*

You will notice we are back to the basic "protocol" of verse five. *God is light and in Him is no darkness at all.* If *God is light* to the very exclusion of all *darkness,* then *fellowship* (partnership) with *darkness* would absolutely exclude any *fellowship with Him.*

Saturate today on this last statement. You were asked to memorize this conclusion in previous studies. Be sure it is clear in your mind for it is dominate in the theme of this epistle.

Day 7

From yesterday's saturation we gleaned the knowledge that there is a condition or state in which we can live which will automatically produce the two results stated in verse seven. The two results are: *we have fellowship with one another*, and *the blood of Jesus Christ His Son cleanses us from all sin*. This gives us the overall view of the verse.

This means that our only concern is to get and stay in the condition. We will quickly see that He is the condition. Our only concern is intimacy with Him. So we want to saturate today in the condition from which the results come. John says, *we walk in the light as He is in the light*.

Day 8

Yesterday we saturated on intimacy with Him which is the only condition necessary to produce the two results as listed in verse seven. John states the condition in verse seven as *we walk in the light as He is in the light*. John is giving us a description of what it means to *walk in the light*. To the same degree *He is in the light* so we are to *walk in the light*

This is the saturation for today. Write this phrase down if necessary. Pray over it asking for insight into the comparison. There is much being said which is in the undercurrent of the phrase.

Write down all the comparisons you can between the state we are to be in and the state of His presence.

Day 9

I trust the Lord inspired you in your saturation from yesterday. John states the condition which produces the two great results found in verse seven. The condition is really the very presence of Christ Himself. John says, *we walk in the light as He is in the light*. You should have a list of comparisons between the two statements *we walk in the light* and *He is in the light*.

Here is a list of possibilities:

> We walk – He is
>
> Time zone – Eternal zone
>
> Progressive (*walk*) – Complete (*is*)
>
> We are in the light – He is both in and is the light
>
> Recipient – Source

Add any new thoughts to your list of comparisons. Saturate on these additions through this day.

We are opening our lives to the condition into which John is calling us. It is going to be the source of everything we desire for our lives. We are not going to concentrate and seek the results; we are going to desire the condition and the results will be automatically experienced. They are strictly a by-product of the condition.

The condition is *we walk in the light as He is in the light.* We are to live in the *light* to the same degree that *He is in the light*. Obviously there is no contradiction between this statement and *God is light and in Him is no darkness at all* (1:5). God not only exists in the *light,* but is the very source of the *light* in which He exists. This reaffirms the absence of all *darkness*.

Therefore, God is not urging us to join Him in living in a certain state or condition. He has not created a building or garden of light which is an atmosphere conducive to His existence and He wants us to live in that building or garden of light with Him. Rather the picture is that of who He is! From God flows the condition of light because He is light. We are being invited to live in what He is or to share in His very nature. For instance, we think of heaven as a place of light. It is a place which will be suitable for us and God to live together forever. John is not talking about this. He is introducing to us the tremendous possibility of deliverance from all darkness through the very source of light becoming the condition in which we live.

You need to saturate of this reality today.

1 John 1:7

Day 11

God is both the source of light and the condition of life. To *walk in the light* is to live in His very nature. John is going to develop this concept throughout this book. He is going to give us a great example of One who *walk*ed *in the light as He is in the light*.

Our saturation today is going to be in the second chapter of this great epistle. I want you to read the first six verses of this chapter. We are going to saturate specifically on verse six, but the context is very important. Obviously the subject is Jesus (2:1). His accomplishment of redemption's provision for us is complete and adequate (2:2). This redemption has brought about an intimacy with Him which can only be stated in "I know Him" (2:3)! Knowing Him brings about a condition of the completion of His Word in us which is completed love (2:4, 5). This kind of intimacy can only be described by *in Him* (2:5). Now John gives us a parallel statement to our saturation condition in verse seven of chapter one. *He who says he abides in Him ought himself also to walk just as He walked* (2:6).

Here is the great example of One who *walked in the light as He is in the light*. Can a human being on this earth in the midst of a darkened world live a life of total light? Jesus is the answer to this question! He walked in the light because He was in the source of the light. Let us *walk just as He walked*.

Saturate on this example today

Day 12

Let's go back and saturate on *as He is in the light* (1:7). Perhaps you feel like we are belaboring the point. If we are, it is worth belaboring. There is no more essential truth in the whole of the Book than the reality of this concept. This must be comprehended or all is lost. The only thing which will keep us from legalism, false expectations (both too high and too low), and doing is the reality of this condition. As you have discovered through saturation, it is Him!

He is not only in the condition of life but He is the source of the light. The degree to which we are to *walk in the light* is Him. Again do not consider walking with Him in the condition of light, rather He is the condition in which you are going to walk. This eliminates all attempts of self-doing. This is the experience of intimacy with Him. We must go after Him and Him alone.

One of the Biblical scholars said, "Walking in the light, as He is in the light, is no mere imitation of God, but an identity in the essential element of our daily walk with the essential element of God's being." John is calling us to experience Him in the fullness of His nature which is light. Spend this entire day focusing on Him. Quote this condition (*walk in the light as He is in the light*) over and over again as you seek Him. Be open to every change He would desire to make in your life!

1 John 1:7
Day 13

As we saturate in the concept of light, we must be careful to realize it is much bigger than what we have comprehended. We must not confine the light to the narrowness of our eyesight. We are being called to *walk in the light* to the same degree that *He is in the light*. We must be aware of the light as it is beyond us.

Consider what Paul said, *He who is the blessed and only Potentate, the King of kings and Lord of lords, who alone has immortality, dwelling in unapproachable light, whom no man has seen or can see, to whom be honor and everlasting power. Amen* (1 Timothy 6:15, 16).

Certainly we are being called to *walk* completely beyond ourselves. How far would you be willing to go in the expanse of the light? What would you be willing to surrender for the sake of experiencing the light? What traditions or customs would you be willing to have altered or eliminated for the wonder of the light being brighter in your life?

Saturate on the greatness of the light today! Allow your heart to respond to its call!

Day 14

We have made a desperate attempt to experience and comprehend what John means when he says **He is in the light**. God is both the source and condition of light. He lives in the light and produces what He lives within. It is His very nature. To the degree He is in this light so we are to *walk in the light*.

We are going to saturate on this concept today. What does it mean to *walk in the light*?

Answer the following questions in your saturation today:

- What does it mean to *walk*?

- Is this *walk* in activities of light or in condition of light? Would it be possible to do all of the activities of light and not be in the condition of light?

- Is this *walk* a progress out of darkness into the shadows into the dawning into the light? Does the light get brighter and brighter?

1 John 1:7

Day 15

I want to review with you our previous saturation on the word *walk* as found in verse six. There is a direct parallel between the two statements *walk in darkness* and *walk in light*. What he is proposing about darkness, he is now suggesting about light. Let me restate our previous saturation on the concept of *walk*.

This is a translation from the Greek word "peripateo." The basic word "pateo" means *to walk*. So our word in the text has the prefix "peri" on it. This has the idea of "around." Notice how the word is used in these following verses:

> 1 Peter 5:8
>
> Galatians 5:16
>
> 1 Thessalonians 2:12
>
> Ephesians 4:1
>
> Ephesians 5:8
>
> Colossians 1:10

Would you not agree that each time in the context of the usage of the word activity is demonstrated? The focus of the word is on movement. The focus of his intent is not on inactivity. In other words, he is not discussing what you do not do or the bad things in which you do not participate. This is not a list of negative and positive rules. This is the general activity of life. Perhaps better stated, it is the atmosphere, bent, or force involved in all of the activities of life.

Take these additional verses above with you throughout the day. Saturate on the context of the word *walk*.

Day 16

In light of yesterday's saturation, let's bring together the two great concepts. We are to *walk in the light* to the same degree *He is in the light*. Let's review what we have discovered.

He is the source of the light as well as the condition of the light. Therefore He is light and is in light at the same time.

The light which He is and is in is significantly greater than our comprehension. So the light in which we are to walk is not knowledge or understanding. We are not expected to "figure out" this condition in which we are to *walk*.

Walk has to do with the source of the total activity of our life. It is not a focus on any single activity but a complete focus on what produces all the activities. God who is light is to be the source of our living which will take us into the realm which we can not comprehend.

In the simplest form, we are being called to intimacy (partnership, koinonia) with Him. Will we live in Him and allow Him to be our source?

If this is not our choice, the only other option is *walk in darkness*.

Saturate on each of these points throughout the day!

1 John 1:7
Day 17

I hope you have reaffirmed your choice to know Him and Him alone. Remember, *God is light and in Him is no darkness at all*. This means that *God is light* to the exclusion of all *darkness*. Therefore any fellowship (partnership) with *darkness* would absolutely exclude any *fellowship with Him*.

John is teaching us that there are two tremendous benefits to living in the *light*.

> *We have fellowship with one another*
> *The blood of Jesus Christ His Son cleanses us from all sin*

What a blessing! When we embrace Him these things begin to take place in our lives. These things are not our focus; He is our concentration. We are amazed at what He is doing within and through us. If we focus on these two things, we will find them slipping from us. He is our focus!

Saturate today on this idea and strengthen the boundaries of your focus!

Day 18

We want to begin our saturation of the first result of our focus on Him, the *light*. *We have fellowship with one another*. We must first of all go back and grasp the idea of *fellowship*. Remember this word is used twice in verse three and now again in verses six and seven. This word is a key to all that John wants to communicate to us.

Let's go back and review this key word, *fellowship*. It is the Greek word "koinonia." You may want to go back into the previous saturation studies and review the details concerning this word. It has the primary meaning of joint-participation with someone else in things possessed in common by both individuals. It was originally focused on the idea of business or an enterprise. The business venture was the common element bringing the individuals together. This is certainly true with our *fellowship* with God. However the joint-participation in common elements between us and God is the common nature we now experience. This gives us common likes and dislikes. From the common nature, a communion of interest and activities which we call *fellowship* takes place. One American Indian language translates this word *fellowship* as "God and I are of one mind."

If we are of the same mind, common nature, with God, what is His nature? This is the "protocol." *God is light and in Him is no darkness at all* (1:5). If *God is light* to the very exclusion of all *darkness*, then *fellowship* (partnership) with *darkness* would absolutely exclude any *fellowship with Him*. It is an absolute impossibility! Thoroughly saturate on this concept today.

Day 19

I am sure you agreed with the saturation of yesterday. *If we walk in the light as He is in the light* one would expect the key result would be we would have *fellowship* with Him. However this is not what John tells us in our verse. He makes a dramatic shift in thought for us. Actually he had suggested this idea in the previous verses. You will note in verse three John states that the message was declared that *you also may have fellowship with us*. But now the message is fully stated. The result of walking in the light is *we have fellowship with one another*.

Darkness is an unsocial condition, and can not be experienced within the light. Again be sure you comprehend the concept of *fellowship*. This is not learning to tolerate each other. *Fellowship* must go beyond this.

There is an issue which must be thought through in relationship to walking in the light. If *fellowship* is joining together in business, becoming partners, and sharing likes and dislikes, we will have difficulty with people of darkness. Is John simply referring to those who are walking in the light? This can easily develop an elitist group which excludes everyone who does not agree with us. There seems to be a distinction between *fellowship* and *love.* *Love* is the inner nature and motive of our personhood while *fellowship* is the embracing of one who has this same nature and motive. We are called upon to *love* people of darkness, but not to have *fellowship* with them.

In light of this issue saturate in Matthew chapter five today. It is the Sermon on the Mount which is the opening manifesto of the Kingdom of God. Saturate in verses forty-three though forty-eight.

Day 20

It is important to notice today the verb tense of this first great result, *we have fellowship with one another.* The verb form is in the present tense. This is to indicate that the reference is to a reality existing at the moment of speaking. *We have* this now.

We are deeply aware that patience is developed and growing in our lives. We learn patience through the trials and tribulations of our lives (James 1:2, 3). But John is discussing the issue of the heart in this statement. Hate and bitterness is a heart issue and is not conquered slowly. It does not become less and less. It must be replaced by the *light. If we walk in the light as He is in the light* there is no room for the darkness of division and dissension.

Our saturation today must be on this issue. Open your life today for the examination of the *light.*

1 John 1:7

Day 21

This theme of being intimate with God (fellowship) and loving one another is a constant thread running throughout this First Epistle of John. Let's continue in our saturation on this subject by viewing some of those Scriptures found in this epistle.

1 John 3:11 – Notice the long duration of the message. In the very next verse John verifies this fact by giving the example of Cain and Abel.

1 John 3:23 – Notice this was the command of Jesus. In the following verse John links "loving one another" with "abiding in Him" as if the two can not be separated.

1 John 4:7 – The reason for loving one another is *for love is of God*. Notice he then again links intimacy with God with this love.

1 John 4:12 - Intimacy with God and loving one another are again linked together. In fact, this is the completion of the love of God!

Dwell on these verses all day long. Let their truth grip you!

Day 22

We are now ready to launch into saturation on the second result of the *walk in the light as He is in the light*. When we are in the condition of the *light*, it results in *we have fellowship with one another*. Now the second result of this condition of *light* is *the blood of Jesus Christ His Son cleanses us from all sin* (1:7).

Let's begin with the overwhelming awareness of this great provision. This great gift of the blood of Christ is absolutely necessary. It is the fulfillment of the substance of the message which John had received (1:5). This message was *that God is light and in Him is no darkness at all* (1:5). If *God is light* to the very exclusion of all *darkness*, then *fellowship* (partnership) with *darkness* would absolutely exclude any *fellowship with Him*.

While this may sound spiritual and right, it leaves us in a place of absolute defeat. There is no chance of living above sin in this world. How could any man claim to live day after day in total victory of sin? Would it not be utterly impossible? Therefore, we are excluded from any involvement with God who is light.

BUT John is coming to our rescue with *the message which we have heard from Him* (1:5). An automatic result of coming into the light is *the blood of Jesus Christ His Son cleanses us from all sin*. Saturate on this provision for you and apply it to your life.

1 John 1:7

Day 23

It must be acknowledged and clearly comprehended that the entire provision God has for us in the *light* is contained in and through the person of Jesus Christ. This calls us back to the complete focus on Him and Him alone. There is no provision outside of His person. This is not something we experience apart from Him, but in Him!

Let's review the whole flow of the verses bringing us to this great truth of verse seven. Verse one is the declaration of what John had heard with his own ears and what he had seen with his own eyes. He had actually handled this *Word of Life*. This is not a doctrine or a new religious creed, but a living person with whom John had interacted.

Now verse two continues with a focus on the manifested life of Christ. Qualities which absolutely stretch the thinking of any person are given to Him. He is eternal and *was with the Father*.

Verse three introduces the startling fact that intimacy may be experienced with those who have seen Him and are declaring the news. But the *fellowship* (partnership) is way beyond us and them and engulfs the Father and the Son. There is a tightness established among us which is all focused on Him.

Verse four points us to the awareness that completeness of joy is found in Him.

The message we are to know and experience is definitely from Him! Verse five reveals the message as *God is light and in Him is no darkness at all*. This is the message of His Person.

Verse six blockades any suggestion that you can be in darkness and have fellowship with Him. Fellowship with Him excludes all darkness.

Now verse seven shares that what seems impossible and far beyond us has actually been provided through the very blood of the One who has been manifested to us and will be intimate with us.

Saturate on the wonder of His person as the provision for you. Be gripped with the fact that every defeat and tolerance of sin is a ridicule of His provision and thus His person. All excuses of allowed darkness turn His provision into a joke.

Day 24

Let's focus today in our saturation upon the Person who is our provision. It is *Jesus Christ His Son*. It is significant to trace this title throughout this epistle. John uses it four distinct times. Each time the Divine antecedent is described differently. In other words, in each case this title is connected and refers to a different aspect of God which gives to us the message He desires to portray.

The first occasion for this title is in verse three of chapter one. John is declaring the message to us that *fellowship* (partnership) may take place. This includes fellowship with those who are declaring the message. The basis of this *fellowship* (partnership) *is with the Father and with His Son Jesus Christ*. In this verse the highlighted relationship is Father and Son. Compare this with the third chapter of the Gospel of John. In the discussion with Nicodemus Jesus highlights this same relationship (John 3:16-18).

The second passage highlighting this title is our study passage (1:7). The second result listed from walking in the light is *and the blood of Jesus Christ His Son cleanses us from all sin*. The relationship is with the One who is light, *God is light and in Him is no darkness at all*. To walk in the light is to experience *fellowship* (partnership) with the "Son of light."

The third passage containing our title is in chapter three. John writes, *This is His commandment: that we should believe on the name of His Son Jesus Christ and love one another, as He gave us commandment* (3:23). This relates back to the statement in verse twenty-one. John is speaking of *God*. Jesus is in relationship with *God*.

The last reference to our title of Jesus is in chapter five. *And we know that the Son of God has come and has given us an understanding, that we may know Him who is true; and we are in Him who is true, in His Son Jesus Christ. This is the true God and eternal life* (5:20). In this great passage, Jesus is related to *Him who is true*.

Thus, John pictures Jesus as related to God as Father, to God as light, to God as God, and to God as the One who is true. It is in Jesus that all of this becomes true for us. His cleansing blood now brings us into this *fellowship* (partnership). Saturate on these things today!

1 John 1:7
Day 25

One specific aspect of Christ which John is highlighting is the *blood of Jesus Christ His Son*. John pictures this aspect as the element which *cleanses us from all sin*. You realize the physical blood of Christ is gone. We do not have a sample of that blood which was shed on the cross for us. Yet it is this very *blood* which is the provision for us!

We want to saturate on the concept of the *blood* today. We must grasp the New Testament meaning as John was using it.

One aspect is that blood is the substantial basis of the individual life. The Old Testament clearly states *for the life of the flesh is in the blood* (Leviticus 17:11). To take the life of an individual, one must take his blood. If you take a person's blood, you have taken his life. Thus the provision of the *blood* is none other than the eternal life of Christ as He was yielded up for us. What a provision! Again notice the focus on the person of Christ Himself.

Another aspect of the *blood* is the Old Testament concept that blood is the material of conception. It is "the bearer of the ongoing life of the species." This clearly underlies the expression John uses in his Gospel. He writes, *who were born, not of blood, nor of the will of the flesh, nor of the will of man, but of God* (John 1:13). This statement is indicating the union of the life bearing blood of both parents in the child. What a concept! The blood of Christ is the seed of life which has brought to birth a new species of beings. They are called "Sons of God." They have the very nature of God which is *light*.

Allow the *blood* (life) of Christ to saturate your life today!

John is establishing a basic holiness concept in these verses. He is going to continue to reveal it throughout the epistle. He places the foundation for this truth firmly in the character of God. It comes from the message which we heard from Christ. *God is light and in Him is no darkness at all*. If *God is light* to the very exclusion of all *darkness*, then *fellowship* (partnership) with *darkness* would absolutely exclude any *fellowship with Him*.

This seems so out of reach to the mind of the average evangelical Christian who seems to want to excuse *darkness* in their lives. John is now giving us the basis for this kind of victory. It is *the blood of Jesus Christ His Son cleanses us from all sin* (1:7). We want to saturate on the idea of *cleanses us from all sin*.

It would help to view another verse where John seems to compare the idea of forgiveness of sin and the cleansing of sin. He says, *If we confess our sins, He is faithful and just to forgive us our sins and to cleanse us from all unrighteousness* (1:9). Obviously these two, *to forgive* and *to cleanse*, are related. But there is a distinction to be noted between the two.

To forgive sins means to remove the sins from someone. Only God is said to be able to do this (Mark 2:10). *To forgive* sins is not to disregard them and do nothing about them. It is not a process of "forgetting" or acting as if they are not there. It is to actually liberate a person from then, their guilt, and their power. We can experience forgiveness from God who removes them away from us so that we do not stand guilty of them or under their power.

To cleanse us from all sin is more than just the removal of the sin and its guilt. In other words, *to cleanse* is more than just the absence of sins. It has to do with purity and sanctification. It is as if something is imparted not just removed from the individual. Forgiveness focuses on *sins* (plural) which are the issue of deeds done. While to *cleanse us from all sin* (singular) is expressed as *to cleanse us from all unrighteousness*. This deals with the very nature of sin which can not be forgiven.

We are only beginning on this subject today. This is going to be highlighted over and over in this epistle as we saturate in its verses. Let these beginning thoughts become clear in your mind today.

Day 27

We are going to focus again today on the idea of *and the blood of Jesus Christ His Son cleanses us from all sin*. How could we possibly go to the depth of this great thought?

Saturate today on the verb tense of *cleanses*. In the Greek language this verb is in the singular, present, active, indicative. Take these thoughts with you today:

Indicative – it is a simple statement of fact. There is no argument and it is not to be discussed. It is simply the way it is. We know the certainty of this statement is found in the life of Christ Himself. This is as sure as God is sure!

Active – this verb is the result of the subject of this sentence. The subject in this part of the verse is *the blood of Jesus Christ His Son*. We receive the cleansing and are a recipient of the very life of Christ. Jesus is solely responsible for this cleansing in our lives.

Present – This tense is the thrust of "now." It is happening at this very moment. However, the present tense expresses duration, and serves to indicate that the cleansing is continuing. This is not a project into the future when we get to heaven. It is not a reflection on what has happened in the past. It is the reality of the very redemptive action of Christ (the *light*) taken place in my life at this moment. As one moment turns into another moment the cleansing is still taking place in the "continuing now."

Day 28

Let's saturate on one more aspect of this great phrase, *and the blood of Jesus Christ His Son cleanses us from all sin* (1:7). We want to focus on the idea of *from all sin*.

The Greek word used here for sin is used often in the New Testament. It has to do with "missing the mark." While in many places it is used to refer to deeds of sin which do not measure up to the moral character of God, it refers in this verse more to the nature of the deed being done. In other words the issue is not the content of the deed itself, but the motive and source of the deed.

This idea is expressed as John continues into the rest of His epistle. For instance, he states, *and you know that He was manifested to take away our sins, and in Him there is no sin* (1 John 3:5). Both *sins* and *sin* are a translation of the same Greek word. However, one is plural and the other singular. The focus of the singular is on the nature of sin itself.

This is further highlight in our verse (1:7) by the use of the word *all*. This is not about the separate manifestations of sin, but the entirety of what is contained within the definition of sin. The deeds in their numerous manifestations and the nature of sin which links all of the deeds together as one are cleansed by *the blood of Jesus Christ His Son.*

Saturate today on these thoughts. Be encouraged to know there is total victory for you in Christ!

Day 29

We are going to spend the last two days saturating on how this verse (1:7) fits into the total message John is conveying to us. In order to do this we must review the outline we have developed so far for this first chapter. If you still have a copy of it carry it with you throughout the day and review the dynamic true which it brings to your mind. If you do not have a copy of the outline please write it on a card and have it available.

I. **Introduction** (1:1-4)
    A. The Person (1:1, 2)
        1. Past to the Present (1:1a)
        2. Physical Testimony (1:1b)
        3. Proclamation (1:2)
    B. The Purpose (1:3, 4)
        1. (of the) Proclamation (1:3)
            a. Partnership with us (1:3)
            b. Partnership with Father (1:3)
            c. Partnership with His Son (1:3)
        2. (of the) Printing (1:4)
            a. Pepleerooménee (1:4)
            b. Pleasurable Contentment (1:4)

II. **The Platform for Fellowship** (1:5-10)
    B. Progression (1:5-7)
        1. Protocol
            a. Perceived (1:5)
            b. Proceeding (1:5)
            c. Proclaimed (1:5)
        2. Pattern of Darkness (1:6)
            a. Presumption (1:6)

b. Peripateo (walk) (1:6)
c. Pseudometha (lie) (1:6)
d. Poieo (do) (1:6)

Notice the first two verses focus on the Person of Jesus. Once we understand His person we know the purpose of the writing which is to have *fellowship* (partnership) with Him (1:3, 4). We immediately begin to understand this *fellowship* (partnership) is on such a high level it must rest on a firm foundation. Therefore in verses five through ten John gives us the platform for the *fellowship*. He begins with the progression of the *fellowship* which is spoken of in terms of the *walk*. The protocol of the *walk* is so strong (1:5). *God is light and in Him is no darkness at all*. Any *fellowship* (partnership) with Him must be in the *light*. We can easily see our *walk* by the pattern in our life. There is the pattern of darkness (1:6). Now we are ready to move to the pattern of light (1:7).

Day 30

We are going to spend our last day of saturation on the verse (1:7) by adding to the outline of the epistle. Remember the purpose of the outline is to give us key words which will prompt our memory of the great truth in which we have saturated.

I. Introduction (1:1-4)
    A. The Person (1:1, 2)
        1. Past to the Present (1:1a)
        2. Physical Testimony (1:1b)
        3. Proclamation (1:2)
    B. The Purpose (1:3, 4)
        1. (of the) Proclamation (1:3)
          a. Partnership with us (1:3)
          b. Partnership with Father (1:3)
          c. Partnership with His Son (1:3)
        2. (of the) Printing (1:4)
          a. Pepleerooménee (1:4)
          b. Pleasurable Contentment (1:4)

II. The Platform for Fellowship (1:5-10)
    C. Progression (1:5-7)
        1. Protocol
          a. Perceived (1:5)
          b. Proceeding (1:5)
          c. Proclaimed (1:5)
        2. Pattern of Darkness (1:6)
          a. Presumption (1:6)
          b. Peripateo (walk) (1:6)
          c. Pseudometha (lie) (1:6)
          d. Poieo (do) (1:6)

3. Pattern of Light (1:7)
     a. Position (1:7)
     b. Partnership Provision (1:7)
     c. Purging Provision (1:7)

There are three major ideas presented to us in the Pattern of Light (1:7). John presents to us a condition which must be true for us if we want the two great benefits he is going to describe. It is simply *we must walk in the light as He is in the light*. From this condition come two significant provisions for our lives. *We have fellowship with one another* and *the blood of Jesus Christ His Son cleanses us from all sin*.

These three ideas must be put in the outline under 3. Pattern of Light (1:7). Remember the issue is not what words you use, but what will remind you of these great truths. Note the suggestions we have put in the outline. Saturate on the over all truth of the verse today as you fill in your own outline.

Word

from

Word

Part Six
1 John 1:8

Day 1

We are launching into the final three verses of chapter one. As you will remember the first four verses of this chapter give us the "Introduction" of the book. It is in this section John highlights the person of Christ and gives us the purpose of the writing of this book. The purpose focuses on "fellowship." This is not "pot-luck supper" fellowship, but koinonia. It has to do with "doing business or "partnership." We are invited to enter into the very enterprise of the heart of God. His greatest desires are being shared with us. We get to participate in His dreams. In fact, we are His dream.

After the "Introduction" John brings us into "The Platform for Fellowship." He explains this in the rest of chapter one. We are going to saturate now in the last three verses of this section. What seems to be so important in the great "Protocol" section is where he "Proclaimed" the fundamental of the entire writing. *This is the message which we have heard from Him and declare to you, that God is light and in Him is no darkness at all* (1 John 1:5). Everything he is going to write in the rest of the book will give content and explanation to this statement. God is light to the exclusion of all darkness. This means any fellowship (partnership) with darkness would absolutely exclude us from any fellowship with Him.

From this basic concept John gives us a "Pattern of Darkness," (1 John 1:6) and then a "Pattern of Light," (1 John 1:7). In other words we begin to see how these two opposing spheres function. It is in view of this that we come into the last three and concluding verses of this section (1 John 1:8-10). You will notice that John introduced the word *sin* at the close of verse seven. It is another word for *darkness*. He is explaining the content of *darkness*. The next three verses are an introductory discussion of this word. Write these three verses on a card and saturate on their content throughout the day.

Day 2

You should be familiar with the content of verses eight through ten from your saturation yesterday. It would be good for you to saturate again today on these three verses. Each verse gives us a basic concept regarding the "Proclamation of Sin." How would you state these concepts? What you select will help us in the formulation of our outline for later.

Keep in mind, John is highlighting the focus on *darkness* which he now states as *sin*. In these verses he is giving us three different perspectives of this subject. What are these three subjects?

Day 3

From your saturation on the last three verses of chapter one, you begin to understand John's concept of *darkness* which he now calls *sin*. You were to state the three aspects of this concept as given in verses eight through ten. Compare your statements with the following:

Verse eight – "Principle" It is here in this verse John declares that *sin* (singular) is much more than just a deed which can be forgiven and forgotten. There is a principle of sin which must be recognized and confronted.

Verse nine – "Particular" The sin principle always produces the **deeds** (plural) of darkness called sins. Those particular sin deeds need to be confessed. They can not be ignored.

Verse ten – "Personal" But this issue of *darkness* must not be viewed as simply "out there." It is a personal issue within our own lives.

Saturate on these thoughts as you add them to what God has revealed to you.

Day 4

Today we are going to saturate on the phrase *If we say*. It introduces the truth of verse eight to us. However from your saturation you no doubt have noticed this phrase is used three times in this section.

Verse six – *If we say that we have fellowship with Him, . . .*

Verse eight – *If we say that we have no sin, . . .*

Verse ten – *If we say that we have not sinned, . . .*

No doubt you remember the study we made in verse six (if not go back and review volume four). Let's review for our saturation today. The word *If* in verses six, eight, and ten is different than in verses seven and nine. It is a translation of the same Greek word, but it has a different usage. In verses seven and nine the force of this conjunction is conditional or hypothetical. In other words, if you meet this certain condition, then these results will be your experience. In verses six, eight, and ten this conjunction is expectational. The emphasis of the word has the meaning of "when" or "whenever." In other words whenever these circumstances or view points are present you can expect this factor to be true. In verse eight, *if we say we have no sin,* then you can expect that you have deceived yourself.

John wants us to look into our lives and see if this is true for us. Take each verse and see if it is true in your life. Saturate on this and let the Lord speak to you.

Day 5

If we say (1 John 1:6, 8, 10) implies that there is someone who is actually saying this. Obviously John is combating with this writing a false teaching which was present in his audience. They believed their sinful conduct or deeds had no affect on their spiritual condition.

Irenaeus (one of the early church fathers) gives a description of this group:

"They hold that they shall be entirely and undoubtedly saved, not by means of conduct, but because they are spiritual by nature. It is impossible that spiritual substance (and by this they mean themselves) should ever come under the power of corruption, whatever the sort of actions they indulged. For as gold submersed in filth, loses not on that account its beauty, but retains its own native qualities, filth having no power to injure gold, so they affirm that they cannot in any measure suffer hurt, or lose their spiritual substance, whatever the material actions in which they may be involved."

We may not believe this perception in its full force. However, could there be any degree to which this fallacy grips us? Saturate on this today.

Day 6

We want to continue in our saturation from yesterday. There is a tension in this section (1 John 1:6, 8, 10) between "saying" and "doing." We speak one thing with our mouths, but our lives are yelling the very opposite. John is telling us that this is not acceptable.

I fear theology and doctrine has a tendency to be removed from the practical aspects of living. Our saturation throughout this book must bring us to total honesty. Any discrepancy between our speaking and our actions must immediately be brought into the power of the *light*.

This demands our attention for this day! Be sure to carefully view the three verses under consideration in light of this pressing need.

1 John 1:8

Day 7

We have been attempting to view our verse (verse eight) in light of its context. Now we need to saturate on it in light of its content.

I am moving into this content with much fear and trembling. There must be no misunderstanding concerning what God is saying to us. Remember saturation is not simply thinking about the verses, but saturating them in prayer to find the mind of God.

The major thrust of this verse is the thought *that we have no sin*. If this is not clearly understood then all else will be misunderstood. We must begin by being sure we are saturating in the passage of the Scriptures. We must not take the passage and place it into our theological bias. We must get into the mind of the writer, his culture, his circumstances, and see his communication. What is he saying to us?

Saturate today in the flow of what the author is saying in light of this key statement. In other words, go back to the basic premise of verse five and walk your way into verse eight with the mind set of the author. Attempt to gain content to what he is referring (*sin*).

Day 8

The major thrust of this epistle is the declaration of the message which he had received from Jesus. It is *God is light and in Him is no darkness at all* (1 John 1:5).

What is the content of *darkness* as seen in opposition to *light*?

What is the synonym for *darkness* which is given to us in verse seven and continued into verse eight?

How does this synonym differ in verse seven from verse eight?

Doesn't verse eight appear to be a contradiction to verse seven?

Saturate on these questions today!

Day 9

Sin is the synonym for *darkness*. John has introduced to us the huge sphere of *light*. It is who God is! It is not an attempt to describe what He does, but the glory of His very being. It will take an eternal life time to discover the full extent of this realm. Anything which is outside of this sphere of *light* is considered *darkness*. *Darkness* is a sphere unto itself. It is far beyond deeds, but contains motive, tone, and most of all source. If it is not being sourced by God it is *darkness* regardless of how good it may appear.

Sin is another word for this sphere of *darkness*. However, sometimes the word *sin* (most often in the plural) is used for the deeds which are so present in the sphere of *darkness*. We must see the word in its right usage. As you saturate in this epistle you must decipher when John is referring to the sphere, realm, or principle of *sin* and when he is referring to the deeds.

With this in mind, saturate again in verse eight. How is the word *sin* being used? See it in light of the surrounding verses.

Day 10

One must not be confused with the statements John is making by taking them out of context. He is attempting to establish a balance in the midst of a culture that wants to go to the far extremes (sound familiar?). In verse seven he distinctly states that *the blood of Jesus Christ His Son cleanses us from all sin*. As we discovered in our saturation on this verse he is speaking of more than just deeds of *sin*. He is equating this with the sphere of *darkness*. We must never be guilty of under estimating the blood of Christ. Total victory and deliverance from *sin* in all of its aspects has been achieved through Jesus' sacrifice. It is important to note this is in the present tense not the future. However, the verse has a sense of duration to it. It is a cleansing that keeps on cleansing. The illustration is that of the coal miner who enters the mine in the morning very clean. He is totally covered in coal soot as he emerges that night. The only clean aspect about him is his eyes. It is not because they have not been bombarded by coal soot but because they have been constantly washed. This is what Jesus is doing for us.

But how does this coincide with the statement John now makes in verse eight? Is it a contradiction?

Saturate on this key issue in this verse.

1 John 1:8
Day 11

Keep saturating on this concept (verse eight) until it is clear in your thinking. This is a crucial issue. Let's attempt to clarify the concepts:

Verse Seven – There is cleansing from and deliverance from all sin through the blood of Jesus Christ. We must not compromise this "victory statement." To lower this standard is to under mind the Gospel and to make a mockery of the cross. Any attempt to allow sin as an acceptable influence on our lives is to make a joke of Jesus.

Verse Eight – We must not go to the extreme of indicating we live in perfectionism. We have never believed in sinless perfection only Christian perfection. We realize we live in a physical world which is under the curse of sin. We realize the soot of the sphere of *darkness* is constantly bombarding our lives. We acknowledge we must have the moment by moment cleansing of the blood of Christ in our lives. Christian perfection as stated by John Wesley is only in the heart, motive of our lives. We have a perfect love for Christ and all rebellion is gone. We are still in a state of needing to pray the Lord's Prayer *"And forgive us our sins, for we also forgive everyone who is indebted to us,"* (Luke 11:4). The sphere of *sin* no longer controls our wills. However, through ignorance and immaturity we are constantly falling short of all God has intended for us. The blood of Christ is constantly cleansing this in our live. There is no sense of arrival or lack of need. We must constantly have the empowering and cleansing of Christ in our lives to have victory over the sphere of *sin* which is present in our world.

Continue to saturate until these distinctions are clear in your heart and mind. Saturate this in prayer as well.

Day 12

Verse eight is strongly focused on the sinful nature which is the sin principle. *Sin* as used in this verse is singular in number and is used without the definite article. All of this is referring to the nature or principle of sin, not acts of sin. However, does not the *sin* as stated in verse seven also include this nature or principle of sin? Yes, it does! Jesus has delivered us from the total nature or principle of sin as well as forgiven us of the total deeds of sin. We no longer need to rebel against God.

Verse eight is encouraging us not to be cocky in this. The sin nature has been cleansed from our heart (the source of life). We are no longer being sourced by this evil nature. There can not be a dual nature of good and bad at war within us. Christ has brought the victory. But it is only in our heart. For years we have been under the influence of the nature of *darkness*. It has developed patterns in attitudes, thoughts, and reactions. While the source has been changed the patterns remain. They are the residue of the old sin nature. Moment by moment Christ is leading us into the revelation of this residue. We are being conformed into His image. All the time this is taking place, we are in perfect *light* for *the blood of Jesus Christ His Son cleanses us from all sin* (1 John 1:7). Continue to saturate on these aspects of verse eight!

1 John 1:8

Day 13

We are continuing to saturate in verse eight. It is very interesting the word *sin* is in the feminine gender. The word *darkness* (verse 5) is in the feminine gender while in verse six it is neuter. In the Greek language the gender of a word is very important. Constantly in this epistle these words are in the feminine gender.

Feminine gender indicates the abstract, immeasurable aspect of the concept. This is contrasted with the masculine gender which is measurable and concrete. In our verse, this again points to the unseen influence and sphere of sin which is all around us. It is not the measurable deeds of sin. We can recognize those and confess them in repentance. But let us not act as if there is not a constant war taking place to defeat us at every point in our lives. Let us not ignore the sphere of *darkness* which would at any moment bring us back under its domination.

Saturate on this and apply it to your life!

Day 14

If we say we have no sin, sphere of darkness, curse of sin in our world, residue of the principle of sin warring against us, what is the result? It is very simple. *We deceive ourselves*.

Most often in the New Testament the verb *"deceive"* is in the passive voice. This states that the subject is being acted upon and is not responsible for the deception. In other words, he is being led astray. But in our verse this verb is in the active voice. This means the subject is responsible for the action of the verb. In other words, by the denial of the sphere of darkness and constant need for Christ's cleansing presence we are acting upon ourselves with deception. We are deceiving no one except ourselves. Everyone else can see the need in our lives, so we have fooled no one except ourselves. Self-deception is never an accident or something beyond our control. It is a direct act of our will. We decide to take the course of least resistance because it protects our self-centeredness. It enables us to side-step the issue of our own spiritual lives.

The discovery of self-deception in your personal life will require painful saturation. Will you do that today?

1 John 1:8
Day 15

We must spend time in saturation on this subject of self-deception as presented in verse eight. One of the most remarkable passages on this subject is found in the narratives of Matthew's account of the Gospel. Take time to read Matthew 27:62-66.

The context is the death of Jesus Christ. His resurrection has not taken place. The leaders of Israel are feeling their personal power in having successfully guarded and protected their religious institution. Notice Matthew makes a strong point to highlight that the action of this passage was on the Jewish Sabbath. He calls it *On the next day, which followed the Day of Preparation* (Matthew 27:62). This underlines how important this action was to the leaders of Israel. They are actually breaking their Sabbath. In order to come to Pilate's palace, they must travel further than a Sabbath Day's journey. Also notice Matthew uses the words *gather together* describe this meeting with Pilate (Matthew 27:62). This means they actually entered the palace of Pilate which they had refused to do on the day of crucifixion. They broke their defilement law by entering a Gentile home. They were willing to do whatever was necessary to secure their concern.

Notice their concern revolved around "deception." Saturate in the passage. See the use of the word. How often is it used? How concerned are they? What was the last deception? What is the first deception?

Day 16

While saturating in verse eight we are viewing an illustration of self-deception found in Matthew's Gospel account. Yesterday we discovered the great concern of the leaders of Israel. They are deeply concerned about deception. Is it not important to notice that our own personal concern for others is most often our own greatest personal need? They have called Jesus *"that deceiver,"* (Matthew 27:63). They consider His ministry while He was alive to be a huge deception. If He is raised from the dead and begins to minister, this would be even a greater deception. Notice they are given a "blank check" from Pilate to do what ever they need to do in order to secure the tomb. Pilate told them, *"Make it as secure as you know how,"* (Matthew 27:65).

Now compare with this passage their reaction to the soldiers who are announcing the resurrection of Christ (Matthew 28:11-15). God has sent a witness to them again. He is giving them one more chance. This witness did not come to them from the disciple community. The Roman soldiers are giving the witness. Note how the leaders of Israel responded to the witness. *When they had assembled with the elders and consulted together, they gave a large sum of money to the soldiers* (Matthew 28:12). *Consulted together* means they came into themselves. They did not seek! They remained in their self-deception. They were willing to lie, bribe, and conceal maintaining their self-deception. Notice in verse fifteen they continued to send representatives everywhere the Christians went in order to spread the deception.

The only way to maintain self-deception is to refuse, block, and eliminate the spreading of *light* in your life. One must fight to maintain *darkness* at all cost. God is constantly attempting to bring us into the full *light* of His revelation. There is nothing more serious than self-deception.

Saturate in this investigation!

Day 17

The leaders of Israel are a perfect example of the explanation of verse eight. They are not seeking, nor are they open. God has brought new light to their lives. The new covenant is at their door (that for which they have been waiting). They chose to maintain where they are. In order to do this they must deceive themselves. It was an attitude of arrival. There was no correction needed in their lives. They were above the need for additional light and truth. Do you see how damning this attitude is to any kind of connection to the *light*?

This is the attitude John is describing for us in his statement, *if we say we have no sin*. If you make any pretense that you have arrived and need no correction, you are living in deception. Don't think for one moment the sphere of *darkness* does not need to be pushed back in your life. It is only by a continual openness to the life of Christ that you can possibly live above sin (1 John 1:7).

I can not stress how essential this is to your personal spiritual victory. Embracing the *light* is not determined by intellectual understanding or mental comprehension. It is only through openness and seeking you can walk in the *light.* The great deterrent to deception, in fact the only deterrent to deception, is seeking. John is striking a blow at this concept in verse eight. This is so serious it demands a continued saturation for this day as well.

Day 18

There is one other aspect of this deception which must be considered. It must be completely understood that John is not using the term to mean "mistaken." This is not a result of ignorance or misjudgment. The word "deception" is used in the strongest sense. This is what makes the whole concept so serious. Even in this first chapter we are seeing the strong contrast. It is *light* and *darkness*. There is **truth** and **deception**. It is as if these are categories and you are in one or the other. John does not picture this as if you can be mistaken about some things but still be in truth. This might be true about some minor issues of theology, but this is not true regarding the issue John is addressing!

When you ignore the sphere of **darkness**, you are engulfed by that **darkness**. If you do not have a healthy fear concerning the influence of this realm upon you, you are already over run with its power. It is in the constantly seeking, openness, hungering and thirsting after righteousness that we find ourselves living in the realm of *light*.

Consider carefully your openness to the *light* as you saturate today.

We are now going to saturate on the last phrase of the verse, *and the truth is not in us*. This is obviously an attempt to summarize the state verse eight is describing. So we need to carefully review and see this statement in light of the whole of the verse.

Remember *if* is not conditional but expectational. It can best be translated "when." When a certain issue is found to be true, you can be assured this circumstance will follow. When you embrace the idea that the sphere of *sin* holds no threat to you, then you are absolutely living in the state of deception. Another way of stating this state of deception is *the truth is not in us*. Understand this is not truth in the sense of certain facts of knowledge, but truth in the sense of *light*.

This echoes again the basic premise of this epistle. *This is the message which we have heard from Him and declare to you, that God is light and in Him is no darkness at all* (1 John 1:5). God is *light* to the exclusion of all *darkness*; therefore any *darkness* excludes us from Him. This is why verse seven is so important to us. *The blood of Jesus Christ His cleanses us from all sin* (darkness). This enables us to *walk in the light as He is in the light*.

In other words, to ignore the sphere of *darkness* is to equally ignore the sphere of *light*. Again it is a call to seeking the *light* (Jesus) with your entire being. Being in the *light* is to be keenly aware that *darkness* is the absence of the *light*. Thus the only chance I have to avoid *darkness* is to run to the *light*.

I am aware we have saturated over and over again on this concept. It is so essential. Be sure it is clear in your thinking as you saturate again today!

1 John 1:8
Day 20

Saturate today on the statement *the truth is not in us*. Be aware that this is a negative statement of the same idea stated in *we deceive ourselves*. Everything which is true about one statement is true about the other. It is a double statement! This tells you how important this truth is to the author. He has a strong desire to communicate this to us. The focus of *we deceive ourselves* is on self-deception. In other words we are not deceiving someone one else or leading them astray, but we are only deceiving ourselves. In fact, others are keenly aware of what is taking place in us. We are the ones who have chosen to ignore the truth. This is true also of the statement *the truth is not in us.* This has nothing to do with anyone else's relationship with the truth, but exclusively focuses of our individual lives.

We deceive ourselves is a voluntary matter. This is not an accident or simple ignorance. We have made a decision and have embraced deception. This is true in regard to *the truth is not in us.* The *truth* has become a lie within us. Again this is not about facts but about *light* (Jesus). There can be no embracing the lie and Him at the same time. One is exclusive of the other. Note there is no third category or middle category in which to hide. John is very strong in placing in either *light* or *darkness*.

Continue to saturate in this concept.

Day 21

As we continue to saturate on the phrase *and the truth is not in us*, recognize that the verb of the statement is in the present tense. It has the idea of continuation in it. It is also in the indicative mood. This means it is a straightforward declaration of fact. There is no argument with this. In other words, as long as we are in the state of denying the sphere of *darkness* which is constantly attempting to influence our lives, there is no truth in us. It is a reality that this will continue as long as the denial continues. As long as we are not open and seeking Him we will have no truth in us.

Saturate today on the concept that the state of "arrival" and the choice of not seeking, perpetuates the elimination of truth within us. What a terrible state in which to live.

Day 22

In our progression of saturation we are ready to look at *the truth*. This is such an overwhelming concept especially as viewed through the eyes of John's writings. It has heavy content. No doubt we will have to do it in a progression. Today, let's saturate on the content of the word *truth* as used in this verse. In the flow of the material, there appears to be a difference between the content of the word in verse six and now in verse eight. While the Greek word used by John is identical, he appears to have a different focus.

You will notice in verse six there is a focus on action. Verse six states *we lie and do not practice the truth*. Here in verse eight the focus is on God's own truthfulness. In other words, any denial of the sphere of *sin* and its influence on our lives is a denial of the truthfulness of God. To act as if we are independent and have no desperate need of the permeating grace of God moment by moment is to violate the truthfulness of God. This is why the Pharisee was so repulsive. At least the publican and harlots knew they had a need. The Pharisee supposed he was above such need.

To help us grasp this truth, let's turn to Luke 18:9-14. Saturate in this passage and apply it to 1 John 1:8.

Day 23

From our saturation yesterday, you gain content to verse eight from Luke's Gospel. No doubt you noticed how specific Luke is to whom Jesus is speaking. It is a parable spoken to *some who trusted in themselves that they were righteous, and despised others* (Luke 18:9). This is the very attitude John is addressing in verse eight. Because of the extreme importance of proper understanding, let me state it again. There are two dominate views which must be kept in tension or balance. On the one side, *the blood of Jesus Christ His Son cleanses us from all sin* (verse seven). On the other side, *if we say we have no sin, we deceive ourselves, and the truth is not in us* (verse eight).

Any form of sin is not acceptable. To give our approval of it, is to weaken the redemption provided by Christ. We must not expect anything less than total absolute victory in this present life. We must expect to live above sin and without its domination in our lives. However, to act like we have arrived in some state where we have no need is to enter back into sin itself. The only reason we have victory at all is because we are constantly receiving His grace and touch on our lives. Any moment we are not seeking and responding to Him we are lost again. To act like there is no desperate need for Him because we have become inoculated against sin is to deny the truthfulness of God. Saturate in this concept as it applies to your own personal life.

1 John 1:8

Day 24

We are continuing in our saturation of the concept of *truth* as given in verse eight. Through the context we have discovered John is referring to God's own truthfulness. Let's go a bit deeper in this concept.

As we go further into the epistle, we will begin to see the strong emphasis on the inner reality of *light* producing the natural expression of living the *light.* He is beginning that idea with this passage. What we see in the person of Christ is the fact that God is truthful. God is truthful because His acting and speaking cover each other completely. If you look at what Christ says (inward), you can find the truth of God. If you look at what Christ does (outward), you can find the truth of God. They are the same.

This is not true for the person who says he has no need. We hear what he says, but are deeply aware of the needs in his life which he is denying. No one is fooled except himself. The truthfulness of God does not abide in him. There is no correspondence between who he is and what he does. He eliminates any possibility of correction or growth. He is no longer seeking.

Saturate in this concept today as it applies to your own life.

Day 25

Let's saturate again on the idea of *truth* as found in verse eight. Remember this is a different context for *truth* than found in verse six. Here John is referring to God's own truthfulness. God's truth constitutes His real being and revealing activities. These two totally match; they are identical. This is really important to us as Christians. God keeps faith with us by doing what He has promised.

Truth in this context has the sense of total both inward and outward. *Truth* has this same content in other verses in:

> 1 John 2:4
>
> 1 John 2:21
>
> 1 John 3:19
>
> 1 John 4:6

Write these verses down on a card and saturate on them throughout the day.

1 John 1:8

Day 26

We have been saturating in the concept of *truth* which is essential in understanding verse eight. We have discovered the focus of this word is on "what God is, is exactly what He does." There is no difference! Obviously this is not true for the person who acts like they have no need.

This gives tremendous content to the person of Christ. Anytime we speak of *truth*, we come back to Jesus. He said, *"I am the way, the truth, and the life,"* (John 14:6). Our very concept of *truth* must be shaped by Jesus. He is the *truth*. Remember Jesus is the *Word* (John 1:1). The very insides of God have been spoken. In Christ we are given the staggering opportunity to compare the insides of God with the external display of His actions. When you look at God's insides and His external actions (Jesus), they are the same. Thus Jesus is the *truth*. If fact Paul states, *He is the image of the invisible God* (Colossians 1:15). He is the marriage of the internal and external of the being of God.

John is calling us to this same marriage. All that God is inside (*light*) must be outside in our actions. Saturate on Jesus today.

Day 27

Perhaps in our saturation today we should look at the application of what we have been discovering concerning *truth*. Remember it is about God's truthfulness. What He is inside and therefore speaks is exactly what He is in His actions. Jesus is the insides of God displayed in outward action. There is no difference between how God feels and how He acts. He is the same in His thinking as He is in His actions.

The application of this is found in the close of verse eight. John states, ***and the truth is not in us***. Put this in the context of the whole verse. If we say we have arrived at a place where we have no need, the sphere of *sin* does not touch us, we are living in deception. The only one we are deceiving is ourselves. Another way of stating this is: ***and the truth is not in us.*** In other words, our inward condition expressed in what we say does not correspond with our outward actions.

In other words, Jesus does not abide in us. You can see how critical John makes this concept. There is absolutely no *darkness* contained in the *light* (1 John 1:5). To state that we have fellowship with Him (*light*) and remain in *darkness* is absurd (1 John 1:6). The reason is that in the *light* (Him) we are cleansed from all unrighteousness by the blood of Christ (1 John 1:7). This shows us how dependent we are on the *light* (Him). We must seek Him, depend on Him, and yield to Him every moment. We are desperate for Him. We are constantly expressing our need and dependency. Any denial of this either inwardly or in our expressed actions nullifies the *light* (Him).

This application of truth requires much saturation today.

Day 28

You will notice in verse eight the conclusion is not just about the **truth**. It is about **the truth** being **in us**. Let's saturate on this phrase **in us**. If you research the writings of John both in his epistles and Gospel, you will discover the content of this phrase. Saturate on the following verses:

John 17:21 – He uses this phrase to express a very close and intimate relationship between Christ and His Father.

1 John 2:5; 5:20 - This same close relationship is stated between men and God.

1 John 4:4 – This verse uses the phrase to express an aspect of God's being with men, or of the devil with the world.

Write these verses on a card and saturate in them today.

Day 29

There is insight to be gained from the Greek word which is translated *in* as found in verse eight. It is the Greek word "en." It has the basic definition of contained within the boundaries of something. However, there is a tone to the word which is very important especially in light of verse eight. It has the primary idea of rest!

This becomes very plain when it is compared with the Greek word "eis." This has the idea of into or unto and implies motion. In other words, it is the idea of actually moving into the boundaries of something. The Greek word "ek" means out of or from and carries the idea of motion out of. So there is "eis" which is motion into and "ek" which is motion out of, but between these two there is "en." This has to do with remaining in place.

Now apply this to our verse (eight). He is not discussing a passing moment or a brief phase through which you are going. This is about the state in which you are abiding. This is about the consistent condition of your heart. One can not state that sometimes I am this way, but not always. This is the constant position in which you abide.

How does this intensify the statement John is making?

Day 30

As we come to a close in our saturation on verse eight, let's place this verse into our outline. Remember the purpose of the outline is to give us handles so we can recall the truth at a glance.

I. Introduction (1:1-4)
    A. The Person (1:1, 2)
        1. Past to the Present (1:1a)
        2. Physical Testimony (1:1b)
        3. Proclamation (1:2)
    B. The Purpose (1:3, 4)
        1. (of the) Proclamation (1:3)
            a. Partnership with us (1:3)
            b. Partnership with Father (1:3)
            c. Partnership with His Son (1:3)
        2. (of the) Printing (1:4)
            a. Pepleerooménee (1:4)
            b. Pleasurable Contentment (1:4)

II. The Platform for Fellowship (1:5-10)
    A. Progression (1:5-7)
        1. Protocol
            a. Perceived (1:5)
            b. Proceeding (1:5)
            c. Proclaimed (1:5)
        2. Pattern of Darkness (1:6)
            a. Presumption (1:6)
            b. Peripateo (walk) (1:6)
            c. Pseudometha (lie) (1:6)
            d. Poieo (do) (1:6)

Word *from* Word

Part Seven
1 John 1:9

Day 1

It is of extreme value to saturate today in the overall view of chapter one. This will help us as we move into a new verse, verse nine. We must see this verse in the flow of what John is attempting to communicate to us.

Fully comprehend again John's great statement concerning the "Person" of Christ (1:1, 2). His proclamation of this person has a great "Purpose" (1:3). It focuses on partnership (koinonia). He then states the purpose of the "Printing" or writing of this epistle (1:4). These verses comprise the introduction to John's epistle.

You must keep this purpose for writing and proclaiming clearly in mind as we move into "The Platform for Fellowship" (1:5-10). He begins by sharing a "Progression" (1:5-7). There is nothing stagnant about this relationship. We are in a constant growth or shrinking pattern. It is all based on the "Protocol" (1:5). This verse should be memorized. It is the theme of the entire epistle. Everything he say must be interpreted in light of this great statement: *God is light and in Him is no darkness at all.* God is light to the exclusion of all darkness. This means any fellowship (partnership) with darkness would absolutely exclude us from any fellowship with Him. This is such a bold statement it requires explanation. John does this by giving us the "Pattern of Darkness" (1:6) and the "Pattern of Light" (1:7). We begin to see how these two opposing spheres function in our lives.

Now we come to our immediate section of study. In the closing three verses of this chapter, John is going to give us insight into the sphere of darkness (1:8-10). At the close of verse seven, he introduced the word *sin* which is another word for *darkness*. He is stating the "Proclamation of

Sin" (1:8-10). The first great truth about sin is the "Principle" (1:8). Do not think for a moment there is not the great sphere of sin which is a constant threat to your relationship with God. This drives us back to the constant need of His cleansing in our lives (1:7). In light of this, we now move to verse nine. Write this verse on a card and saturate on how the truth of this verse expands your understanding of *sin*.

Day 2

From your saturation of yesterday, you should grasp a new aspect of sin. No doubt you noticed John has shifted from *sin* (1:8) to *sins* (1:9). This is a move from sin as a principle or sphere of darkness to individual, particular deeds of sin. This highlights the two-fold facet of sin. There is the nature or principle of sin and the result or deed of sin. According to verse seven, the blood of Jesus *cleanses us from all sin* which would include both facets. It is vital to understand this from the platform of verse eight. We must never think we have arrived in a position where *darkness* is no longer a threat. Christ does not place us in a protective bubble where the sphere of sin does not have access to us. Our only victory is in the moment by moment cleansing of His blood within us.

However, we must not treat *sin* as if it is sphere of darkness which only affects the world around us. We have participated in that realm by the very sinful deeds of our life. This verse is placing our focus on those deeds. Take a card upon which to make notes. Saturate all day on what this verse is saying about your particular deeds of sin.

1 John 1:9

Day 3

No doubt you have now perceived an overall view of this verse! We want to take that view and deepen it by examining each aspect of this verse.

Note there is a beginning focus on us in the verse, *If we confess our sins*. Then there is a larger focus on Him in the rest of the verse, *He is faithful and just to forgive us of our sins and to cleanse us from all unrighteousness.*

I want you to saturate today of the interaction of Christ with us at every step of the process. John's call to us throughout the proceeding verses is to *walk in the light*. This *light* does not start with *the blood of Jesus Christ His Son cleanses us from all sin*. The very ability to be aware of our sins is a result of the sphere of light. How would we know that we are in *darkness* if we had not seen the *light*? It is the *light* which brings us to the place of response and confession. This is called "prevenient grace." Calculate the intervention of the *light* in your life!

Day 4

It is very important (as we have noted in proceeding studies) that John begins verse nine with *If*.

No doubt you remember the study we made in verse six and reviewed in verse eight (if not go back and review volume four). Let's review for our saturation today. The word *If* in verses six, eight, and ten is different than in verses seven and nine. It is a translation of the same Greek word, but it has a different usage. In verses six, eight, and ten this conjunction is expectational. The emphasis of the word has the meaning of "when" or "whenever." In other words whenever these circumstances or view points are present you can expect this factor to be true. In verses seven and nine the force of this conjunction is conditional or hypothetical. In other words, if you meet this certain condition, then these results will be your experience.

Apply this to verse nine. Note what it does to the tone of the entire verse. Saturate on this today.

Day 5

There is another view concerning the "if-clause" of verse nine. This will give you additional insight into what John is relating to us. From verse six of chapter one through the first verse of chapter two, there are six "if-clauses."

Three of these are false deductions which one could draw from the belief that *God is light*. Some believe that the claims represented in these false deductions may be slogans or summaries of the position of false prophets/teachers trying to affect the fellowship of believers. Let me list these three:

Verse six – We walk in darkness, but we have fellowship with God.
Verse eight – We have no sin.
Verse ten – We have never sinned.

The conclusion of each of the false assumptions is:

Verse six – We are liars and do not practice the truth.
Verse eight – We deceive ourselves and the truth is not in us.
Verse ten – We make Him a liar and His Word is not in us.

Saturate on these false assumptions as a base for under-standing verse nine. See the connection between each one of them.

Day 6

No doubt from yesterday's saturation you saw a definite progression in the three false assumptions. He begins with the false idea that one can have fellowship with God and still walk in darkness. You can see at the heart of this false assumption there is a voluntary deception. This must lead one to assume that sin has no affect on your life. In other words, sin does not matter. The sphere of darkness has no influence on your life. The next step is to forget what you have been and done. It is one thing to be forgiven and another thing just to forget. Therefore, you act as if you have never sinned. But note it is all a result of deception.

Note the opposite of this blind deception is to be open as in verse nine. It is our only chance to walk in the light. Saturate on this openness.

1 John 1:9

Day 7

Remember three of these are false assumptions. It is almost as if John is quoting the slogans or emphasized statements of certain individuals who are trying to influence his people. Let me list again the three false assumptions:

Verse six – We walk in darkness, but we have fellowship with God.
Verse eight – We have no sin.
Verse ten – We have never sinned.

The conclusion of each of the false assumptions is:

Verse six – We are liars and do not practice the truth.
Verse eight – We deceive ourselves and the truth is not in us.
Verse ten – We make Him a liar and His Word is not in us.

Now to each of the false assumptions, John advances a truth counterclaim:

Verse seven – We do walk in the light as He is in the light.
Verse nine – We confess our sins.
Verse one of chapter two – We may not sin, but if we do there is provision.

The conclusion of each of the truth counterclaims is:

Verse seven – We have fellowship with one another, and the blood of Jesus cleanses us from all sin.
Verse nine – He is faithful and just to forgive us and to cleanse us.
Verse one of chapter two – We have an Advocate with the Father.

Saturate on these counterclaims today.

Day 8

From your saturation yesterday you no doubt discovered there are two parts to each counterclaim. John begins by refuting the claim that sin is no problem and does not affect me. Second, he boldly states the importance of the person of Christ in relationship to my sin.

Let's view the first section of the "if-clauses" (1:6, 7). In verse six someone is claiming to have fellowship (koinonia – partnership) with God and yet is walking in darkness. Obviously this person is a liar and is deceiving them self as well as others. The counterpart to this is verse seven. We actually are walking in the light as He is in the light. But this is true only because of the blood of Jesus Christ His Son Who is constantly cleansing us from all sin. The person of Jesus is constantly dealing with the sin problem which would destroy our lives.

Let's view the second section of the "if-clauses" (1:8, 9). In verse eight, we boldly state that we have no problem with sin (sphere of darkness). We act as if we are beyond it which is self-deception. The counterpart to this is verse nine. We are constantly open and seeking. We are always admitting our need. It is in this openness we can experience the forgiveness and cleansing of Christ.

Let's view the third section of the "if-clauses" (1:10; 2:1). In verse ten, we look at our past and deny that we have sinned. Again this is a state of deception. The counterpart to this is the first verse of chapter two. While it is true we may live without sin, let's not foolishly state that we have done so. Let us constantly rely on our Advocate, Jesus Christ the righteous.

Saturate on these truths today.

1 John 1:9

Day 9

In saturating on the three sections of the "if-clauses" (no doubt) you noticed the relationship between the openness, seeking, and confessing sin and the person of Christ. Indeed, these two are integrally related.

Realize this great truth today! When one denies sin, one must deny the need for Christ's atonement. If you treat sin lightly in your life, you are likewise treating the sacrifice of Christ lightly. If you advocate that you can walk in darkness (sin) and still have fellowship with God, you are boldly declaring that the blood of Christ is not necessary or did not accomplish the task of giving victory over the one thing which keeps us from fellowship (koinonia – partnership) with God. The strength of sin which we have committed in the past and is attempting to influence our lives in the present is measured by the strength of the blood of Christ.

We must treat sin seriously or belittle the work of Christ. Apply this to your life today.

Day 10

We want to continue in our saturation by focusing on the words of our verse. Notice John writes, *If we* (1:9). He has included himself in this statement. You might start at the beginning of this chapter and view the dominate use of the pronoun. You will note the tone that this suggests. He goes on in chapter two verse one to state, *My little children.* We must never see John as condemning or wagging his finger at us. He is identifying with us. He knows where we are and what we are experiencing. He is deeply aware of the needs of our lives for he is a part of us.

In our own spiritual relationship with others, this is extremely necessary. How often we have the "them" and "us" mentality. We come to church and pray, "Oh Lord, there are people here today who desperately need you." Does this not imply that we do not need Him? Focus on your life today. What is the tone or attitude of your approach to others?

Day 11

We are going to focus on the word *confess* today. It is very important for us to understand the concise meaning of this word. It comes from basically two Greek words. The first is "homos" which means "together with" or "one and the same." The second word is "legoo" which means "to say."

There are three usages of this word in the New Testament. You need to have a thorough understanding of these in order to grasp the depth of what John is saying in this verse. We will saturate on the first meaning today.

This Greek word translated *confess* is used to mean "to assure," "to promise," or "to concede." Look up the following verses and write them on a card to saturate on the usage of this word.

Matthew 14:7 – Herod Antipas made a promise to his mistress concerning the dancing of her daughter.

Acts 7:17 – God had made a promise to Abraham concerning his seed.

Hebrews 6:13 – It is again a reference to the promise God made to Abraham.

This Greek word is used to "bind the speaker to his word." Saturate on the strength of this word. This is not light or superficial. This is not "well I may have done some things wrong." This proposes a total ownership between my sins and me. There is no blame on anyone but me. I am bound to the sin I have committed.

Day 12

Don't forget the saturation from yesterday. Today we are going to continue in our focus on *confess*. There are three usages of the word in the New Testament. One is the idea of "to assure," "to promise," or "to concede." The speaker is binding himself to his word. Let's go to the second usages of this word. It is "to make a statement" or "bear witness" in a legal sense. In the Gospel tradition this becomes the most important usage of the word. Saturate on the following verses by writing them on a card and viewing them throughout the day.

Luke 12:8 and Matthew 10:32 – These two verses establish the linkage between heaven and earth. What we say about Jesus down here influences what is being spoken about us in the heavens.

In our passage the confession is about our sins. It is a spoken word which binds us to what we have done and openly exposes it to heaven. It will be spoken everywhere.

Day 13

We are continuing our saturation of the word *confess.* Remember it is two Greek words placed together. It has to do with "homos" which means "one and the same" and "legoo" which means "to say."

It is used three ways in the New Testament. It is used as a promise which means I am bound to my word. In the confession of sins there is a bind of myself to those sins. I openly embrace them. It is also to indicate a connection between what I am giving myself to here on earth and what is being reflected about me in the heavenly realms. In relationship to the confession of my sins, I am not only binding myself to my sin but I am declaring it before the heavenly realms.

The third usage of the word in the New Testament is "to make solemn statements of faith" or "to confess something in faith." Write Romans 10:9, 10 on a card and saturate in it for this day. Understand this connection with the confession of sins. By confessing my sins, I am admitting I am bound to them because they are mine. I am opening declaring them before all of the heavenly realms. I believe in all that is provided in the rest of our study verse (1 John 1:9).

Day 14

Let's spend one more day saturating on the idea of *confess*. It is significant that the phrase "confess our sins" does not appear anywhere else in the New Testament. We are going to find over and over again that John in this epistle is going to be uncompromising. He loves and is kind but will not pamper us. It is because of the seriousness of the theme of this book. *God is light and in Him is no darkness at all* (1 John 1:5). This means that *God is light* to the exclusion of all *darkness*. Any fellowship with darkness immediately excludes us from fellowship with God.

If the *blood of Jesus Christ His Son cleanses us from all sin* (1:7), we must boldly and completely confess. We must not hesitate or timidly confess. We must not only be deeply aware of the sphere of darkness pressing upon us, but we must be open about the effects which have resulted from it. We are to take sides with God against ourselves.

As you saturate on this today, embrace this truth. State to yourself and to Him over and over again, "I am taking sides with you, Jesus, against myself."

Day 15

There is one other aspect about the issue of *confess* we must not miss. Let's saturate on it today. It is the verb tense of the word. This verb is in the present, active, subjunctive. This means that it indicates continuous action. It could be translated like this "if we keep on confessing our sins."

We are not indicating that we should continue to confess the same sin over and over again. But John is speaking about the sphere of darkness or the effects of it as demonstrated in our lives. We are to have a constant attitude of a contrite heart which is ever eager to have any sin in our lives discovered and revealed by the Holy Spirit. In other words, every thing we have learned about *confess* in the last several days is to be a constant state. *Confess* is not to be a simple act in a moment, but a life style in His presence.

Saturate on applying this to your life today.

Day 16

To complete the opening phrase of this verse (1:9) John places the words *our sins*. The Greek word translated *our* literally means "of" or "from us." This is very personal and particular.

I find it easy to go to church and in a large congregation repeat responsively, "we have all sinned." Everyone will admit that they are not all they should be. Often someone will be justifying themselves and will quickly add, "Not that I am perfect!" But to embrace Him, is to embrace everything He is saying about my personal, particular sins.

This again brings us to the issue of ownership. I must see them coming from me and produced by me. They are mine. I can only *confess* those that belong to me.

Apply this to your life today through saturation.

1 John 1:9

Day 17

We have saturated on the word *sins* in previous verses. But it will help us to look at it again today. The entire focus of our confessing is to be upon *sins*. We are to be continuing in the attitude of confessing *sins*. It would certainly be important for us to know to what we are referring.

The Greek word translated *sins* means "missing the mark." In the Biblical context John is referring to everything which misses the true end and scope of our lives, which is Christ. In other words, every deed of our lives must be viewed in light of the Person of Christ. How does this deed relate to Christ and my relationship with Him? You can easily see this is not something to do and have done. There must be a constant openness and examining of every act of life in light of His Presence.

Saturate on applying this to your life.

Day 18

In our saturation today we are going to move into the next great statement in this verse. *He is faithful and just!* It is absolutely essential to understand these two concepts (*faithful* and *just*) in order to understand the results of our confession.

The Greek word for *faithful* is "pistos." The Greek word for *believes* (John 3:16) is "pisteuoon." You can see that it is the same basic word. In other words, what God is in His own nature is exactly what He is wanting out of us. Saturate on this for today. Think about what God is calling us to in this great epistle of 1 John as we have studied so far.

God is light and in Him is no darkness at all (1:5). This is the nature of God; He wants us to have this same nature.

Day 19

The Greek word for *faithful* means "true, sure, trustworthy, and believable." It has to do with being worthy of credit. In other words, you can depend upon Him. As you place this meaning into the verse, it changes your view of what is being said. When you first study the verse, one would think in terms of conditions. *If we confess our sins* is a conditional statement. God does not forgive or cleanse unless we *confess*. This gives the picture of God sitting back waiting on us before He acts in our behalf. Of course, we know this is not true. Faithfulness is His character and nature. The Biblical truth is that He has forgiven you whether you *confess* or not because it is His nature. This is the way *light* is! Confessing our sins simply puts us in the position where we can receive that which God has already done.

The nature of God does not change with your confession. He is the same regardless of what you do. He is acting the same towards you whether you *confess* or not. The change is not in Him but in you and me! God is constant (*faithful*) in His character. This is why we can trust Him.

Let this truth become reality for you today through saturation.

Day 20

It would be of value for you to saturate today on the various issues of God's faithfulness as found in the Scriptures. This will give content to our verse. Write these verses down and saturate on them today.

Hebrews 10:23 – His own promises.

1 Thessalonians 5:24 – In the fulfillment of the calling or purpose for your life.

1 Corinthians 10:13 – In giving you victory over temptation.

2 Timothy 2:13 – In His character and nature.

1 John 1:9

Day 21

It is necessary today to summarize our saturation on God's faithfulness as seen in our verse. We do not want to get sidetracked from the truth John is sharing with us.

Forgiveness and cleansing is ours from God. It is because of the very nature of God. He is *faithful*. You can never touch Him without experiencing *light*. The reason is **God is light and in Him is no darkness at all.** God does not give *light* when we approach Him. He is *light* and we discover it when we experience Him. So it is with forgiveness and cleansing. It is His nature to be redemptive. When we *confess* we are discovering the true, constant character and nature of God. He does not change because of our confession. We experience Him because we have confessed. Confession removes the barriers within us which allow the embrace.

Saturate on this focus today.

Day 22

You have noted that the word *just* is connected to the fact that God is *faithful*. These two words imply each other. We want to saturate on the concept of *just*. It is often translated "righteous." For instance, view 1 John 2:1.

It means that someone is conforming in his actions to his nature. The rules are self-imposed. I want you to see the contrast between who we are and who God is. Romans 3:10 gives us this picture. Write this verse on a card for the purpose of saturation. This may be something you need to confess (remember the meaning of the word). No individual in his behavior has fulfilled the expectations of God in his life. We have been conforming to our own nature which is the sin principle.

Saturate on the contrast between God's justice and ours.

1 John 1:9

Day 23

Perhaps it would be well in our saturation today to clearly state the distinction between the righteousness of God and the righteousness of man. Remember that the word *just* is also translated "righteous."

God is *just* which means He always does what is in accordance with His own will or nature. His nature is "faithfulness." He is consistently doing what He is! This is why the rest of verse nine is so forceful. Forgiveness and cleansing are redemptive acts. God can not do anything but be redemptive.

However, when this word is related to man, there is a change. It means that man is being or doing what is right in God's eyes or living according to God's will. We can quickly see that we have no chance of "righteousness" outside of Him. Saturate on this thought today.

Day 24

There are two bold statements in the verse which we are studying. *If we confess our sins* certainly has a focus on us. However, remember it is only because of Him that *light* has revealed the *darkness* of our lives. So in reality even our confession is a result of His grace.

The second part of this great verse is a focus on the character and nature of God. *He is faithful and just to forgive us our sins and to cleanse us from all unrighteousness.* This great section of the verse is divided into two major sections. First, there is *He is faithful and just*. Second, there is *forgive us our sins and to cleanse us from all unrighteousness*. You will note the link between these two sections is *to*. This is a very significant word in the Greek language and becomes the pivotal point of these two phrases.

John in his writings seems to give special meaning to this word. He almost always uses it to express purpose. It can be translated "in order that." *He is faithful and just* is a total focus on the nature of God. *Forgive us our sins and to cleanse us from all unrighteousness* is a focus on the natural results of that nature. There is an additional insight connected to this Greek word translated *to*. It has to do with finality. When this word is used in John's writing, it is as if that is the end of the discussion. Saturate today in the certainty we have when we come to Him in confession!

1 John 1:9

Day 25

We begin today to saturate on the concept of "forgiveness." Remember this is an expression and a direct result of the nature of God. He can not do anything but forgive. Let's saturate today on the very meaning of the word *forgive*.

The Greek word translated *forgive* means "to send away." There is a dismissal on the part of one who has been offended. It is like a debt that has been "put away." The Greek word is a basic root word with a prefix. The prefix is the preposition "apo." It refers to something around or near by. This is in contrast to the Greek word "ek" which refers to "inside." The basic root word means "to send." Thus the word *forgive* means to cause our sins to stand away from us or to free us from them in such a way that we will not repeat them and we are not held guilty for them. They are no longer inside us but apart from us.

Saturate on this great truth today. Let it grip your heart and life!

Day 26

The "forgiveness" proposed in our verse and in chapter two, verse twelve are the same. There seem to be three major types or categories for the usage of this word *forgive*.

1. The first is based on the attitude or action of the one who forgives. In the case of our verse, it is the God who is **Light** who forgives. This means the one who forgives "loses sin from his heart" or "does not remember the sin."

2. The second is based or focuses on how the sin is handled. It has the idea of "to carry away sins." It indicates a removal of the sin itself.

3. The third is based on legal terminology. It has to do with justice. It means "to remit the punishment for sins."

Saturate on these three great ideas as they apply to our verse!

Day 27

Today in our saturation we want to link with the idea of *forgive* the startling idea of *cleanse*.

Let's begin by recognizing the verb tense of these two great actions of God. To *forgive* is in the aorist tense. To *cleanse* in grammar is identical in every way to *forgive*. The aorist tense is a focus on a completed action. In other words, this is not a process, but a single accomplished act.

Note this is in contrast to the "cleansing" stated in a previous verse (1:7). John states, *"And the blood of Jesus Christ His son cleanses us from all sin."* This is a present tense indicative (statement of fact). This is a focus on the duration of the action, in other words He "keeps on continually cleansing."

What a statement of victory has been given to us. In a completed act, God will *forgive* and *cleanse*. We can consider it accomplished. At the same time He will continually guard and *cleanse* us from every aspect of sin which would ensnare us. He is our present and continual victory over sin.

Saturate on this truth today!

Day 28

Today we will saturate on the meaning of *cleanse*. It needs to be clearly understood in its connection with *forgive*.

It would be good to review the three usages of the word *forgive* as seen in the New Testament (Day Twenty-Six). Could it be that John does not want any misunderstanding? He is now clarifying the content of forgiveness. Yes, in the mind and heart of God the sin offense has been removed and forgotten. Yes, the punishment of sin has been absolved. But, let it be clearly and completely grasp that God is doing something in the heart of the "confessor." The pollution of sin itself is removed from the life of the believer! Not only does God forgive the believer, but He cleanses him from the defilement which is deepened in his life through the committing of the act of sin.

Bask in the cleansing of God in your life throughout the day!

1 John 1:9

Day 29

As we come to the end of verse nine the phrase *from all unrighteousness* needs to be considered. There is a distinct connection between the word *just* and the word *unrighteousness*. The word *just* is "dikaios" which comes from the root word "dike" which is "right." The word *unrighteousness* is "adikias" which comes from the same root word.

God is absolute rightness. He must be faithful to His own nature. Through the ***blood of Jesus Christ His Son*** He has made a way to bring us into His nature. Remember ***God is light*** (righteous). His design for us is that we would be partners (fellowship – koinonia) with that *light*. He has not failed in His design or action. His dream has been accomplished.

Don't let anything rob you of this accomplishment. The fulfilled dream of God for your life is your resting place.

Day 30

As we come to a close in our saturation on verse nine, let's place this verse into our outline. Remember the purpose of the outline is to give us handles so we can recall the truth at a glance.

I. Introduction (1:1-4)
    A. The Person (1:1, 2)
        1. Past to the Present (1:1a)
        2. Physical Testimony (1:1b)
        3. Proclamation (1:2)
    B. The Purpose (1:3, 4)
        1. (of the) Proclamation (1:3)
            a. Partnership with us (1:3)
            b. Partnership with Father (1:3)
            c. Partnership with His Son (1:3)
        2. (of the) Printing (1:4)
            a. Pepleerooménee (1:4)
            b. Pleasurable Contentment (1:4)

II. The Platform for Fellowship (1:5-10)
    A. Progression (1:5-7)
        1. Protocol
            a. Perceived (1:5)
            b. Proceeding (1:5)
            c. Proclaimed (1:5)
        2. Pattern of Darkness (1:6)
            a. Presumption (1:6)
            b. Peripateo (walk) (1:6)
            c. Pseudometha (lie) (1:6)
            d. Poieo (do) (1:6)

Made in the USA
Middletown, DE
24 June 2019